Scot Lehigh

The Media Show

The Media Show

The Changing Face of the News, 1985–1990

Edwin Diamond

The MIT Press
Cambridge, Massachusetts
London, England

To Justine, Jared, Leah, Chloe, Sasha, and Ethan, who take us into the 21st century.

© 1991 Massachusetts Institute of Technology

All rights reserved. No part of this book may be reproduced in any form by any electronic or mechanical means (including photocopying, recording, or information storage and retrieval) without permission in writing from the publisher.
This book was set in Bembo by The MIT Press and was printed and bound in the United States of America

Library of Congress Cataloging-in-Publication Data

Diamond, Edwin.
  The Media Show : the changing face of the news, 1985–1990 / Edwin Diamond.
    p. cm.
  Includes index.
  ISBN 0-262-04125-1
  1. Television broadcasting of news—United States. 2. Mass Media—Political aspects—United States. 3. Mass Media—Social aspects—United States.
I. Title.
PN4888.T4D478 1991
302.23'45'0973—dc20   91-16835
                                                                                   CIP

Contents

Introduction ix

Structures

1
Televison under *Glasnost*: Letterman Meets Lenin 3

2
Downsizing the News 11

3
Behind the Peacock Throne 19

Face of the News

4
The Vanishing Documentary 29

5
Anchor War 37

6
CNN: The News on Demand 55

7
The Education of Diane and Sam 65

Case Studies

8
AIDS, Sex, and "Good Taste" 1: Practicing Unsafe Journalism 75

9
AIDS, Sex, and "Good Taste" 2: Celebrity Journalism 87

10
High on Crack 93

11
Race, Class, and Crime 1: The Brawley Mess 101

12
Race, Class, and Crime 2: The Central Park Jogger 113

13
Romancing the Don 123

14
Terrorvision: Taking the Camera Hostage 129

15
Seeing Red: Images of the USSR 139

16
Mistaken Identities: The United States and Japan 153

17
The Unknockables 161

18
Gotcha!: The Media as Moral Police 173

19
Campaign '88: Onward and Downward 183

20
The Yawn of a New Day 189

Perestroika

21	The Incurious Eye	197
22	The Camera Never (Admits that It) Blinks	205
23	You Saw It Here First	213

Index 219

Introduction

In the period leading up to the fall of the Berlin Wall in November 1989—a symbolic event given global resonance by its live occurrence before millions of world television-watchers—the old geopolitical notion of convergence has taken on pointed new meanings. The Soviet Union and its erstwhile Eastern European satellites have begun to embrace parliamentary elections, multiparty politics, expanded civil liberties, and other features of Western democracies. Meanwhile, certain trend lines in the West have been equally dramatic, if more disturbing. In the United States in particular the erratic course of corporate mergers and acquisitions at times suggests that the world's oldest democracy is moving toward bigger and bigger conglomeration—and the creation of the same kind of blundering monoliths that the communist bloc has been fleeing.

What in the world is going on?

My discussion of the Eastern Europe's apparent embrace of democratic multiplicity is tentative, as is that embrace itself. The subtitle of my first chapter, "Letterman Meets Lenin," is of course metaphorical; the reporting was developed during two recent visits to the Soviet Union, one in the winter of 1989 and the other in the spring of 1990. I plan to explore further changes in Soviet media over the next few years. Meanwhile, I feel myself on stronger ground analyzing the effects of changes in media ownership in the

United States, as well as commenting on the present practices of the American television news system. The merger and acquisitions game on Wall Street slowed as the decade of the nineties began; this may be temporary, a pause to give the pythons time to digest their meals, or it may signal the outbreak of sanity in the country. But don't bet on it, as they say on The Street.

The most visible examples of American media conglomeration have been evident since 1985 in commercial broadcasting. NBC is now just one of the many holdings of the General Electric Company; ABC was acquired by Capital Cities Broadcasting; and control of CBS shifted from its founding father William S. Paley to Laurence Tisch, who also owns insurance and tobacco companies. These new owners have introduced more "businesslike" procedures in commercial broadcasting; the annual budgets for their network news divisions, for example, have been reduced from highs near $300 million in the mid-1980s to levels of around $250 million in 1990. The old-line networks cut their news budgets in part in response to lowered revenues stemming from increased competition: from the new Fox television network owned by Rupert Murdoch, from Ted Turner's Cable News Network (CNN), and from other cable television operators. Conglomeration has a good side: the arrival of Murdoch, Turner, et al. means that there are more players in the game now. If our media are owned and our popular culture is shaped by monoliths, it helps that there are more of them around today (at a minimum, to get in each other's way).

Beyond the budget numbers, it is more difficult to measure recent qualitative changes in broadcast journalistic performance. Critics have tended to look in the direction of possible "tampering" with news content. As of now, the monoliths have been careful; NBC News's attention to developments in China, for example, has proceeded independent of any GE desire to sell heavy-turbine machinery to Beijing. In other popular media, the picture is still developing. Sony of Japan has acquired Columbia studios in Hollywood. Matsushita, also of Japan, bought MCA, Inc., which includes Universal studios. Pathe Communications, controlled by Italian interests, now owns MGM/UA. In addition, Pioneer Electronics of Japan, manufacturers of Laserdisc players, owns a share of Carolco Pictures, and JVC, the Japanese developer of the VHS home-video format, has invested in Largo Entertainment. These all represent the merger of so-called hardware and software activities. The economic rationale holds that a steady stream of motion picture and television "product" is needed to guarantee that the *on* buttons of VCRs and television sets stay lit. But what will those screens show? Will films like *The Last Emperor* continue to be made in the future without substantial changes? When the chairman of Matsushita was asked about guarantees of creative freedom for his new properties, he professed not to understand why his questioners were worried.

In truth, there is no need to invoke foreign villains in the emerging media dramas of our day. In the late 1980s the Newhouse family of New York purchased Random House, the distinguished book publisher. The new owners forced the resignation of Random House chairman Robert Bernstein and also pushed out Andre Schiffrin at Pantheon Books, a Random House imprint. According to supporters of the two publishers, Bernstein and Schiffrin's crime was their devotion to "intellectual" books that failed to produce adequate revenues for the Newhouse empire. S. I. Newhouse has chosen so far not to reply to his critics: his is a privately held company, and therefore he is not accountable to stockholders or market analysts. But today, even the heads of public companies may operate beyond the pull of public opinion. The cultural megadeal of the 1980s involved Time Inc. and Warner Communications. Their merger brought together magazines, book publishing, motion pictures, video, and other informational and entertainment activities. The announcement of the deal spoke of the "economies of scale" that would result. The public relations releases left out perhaps the most significant fact: Time Inc. executives sought the Warner deal principally because their company had become a target of other, hostile, would-be acquisitors. The upbeat talk about the great operational "synergies" growing from the merger came later.

In the old Time Inc. started by Henry Luce, the magazines were the centerpiece of the company, and the focus of the founder's intellectual energies, for good or bad. Today, from the lofty point of view of Time-Warner management atop their $15 billion company, the magazines have become merely one of several product lines. Critics' fears that these magazines might lose some of their independence were hardly eased when *Time* magazine, the oldest and largest of the Luce publications, devoted its cover story of 11 June 1990 to the new novel by author Scott Turow. To that point, such recognition had been accorded to only a handful of other novelists in the 67 years of *Time's* existence (among them, Ernest Hemingway, Aleksandr Solzhenitsyn, and John Updike). The paperback rights to Turow's book belonged to a Time-Warner imprint, and the motion picture version of his first novel, *Presumed Innocent*, was due out the next month—from another Time-Warner company. *Time* editors maintained that their critical judgments would never be influenced by corporate interests; their argument had a certain plausiblity, although it might have helped if the article had forthrightly dealt with the Time-Warner connections.

Time marches on, indeed . . . toward an uncertain destination.

The period 1985 to 1990 is covered in these narrative reports, from approximately the start of the second Reagan administration through the beginning of the breakup of the Soviet Empire. Almost all of the chapters center on news and public-information formats in the United States. In the first section, Structures, I consider some of the consequences of the new order created by higher technologies and lowered aspirations. Portable television cameras on the ground and satellites in the sky now ensure that major events occurring anywhere in the world can be transmitted to audiences watching their TVs anywhere else in the world. This was demonstrated, breathtakingly, on 16 January 1991, the first night of the Gulf War, when American television viewers were riveted to their sets by the audio reports of a team of CNN correspondents in Iraq. The CNN team was able to broadcast live from an observation post in the Al-Rashid hotel in downtown Baghdad during the allied air attacks. In the following days the same CNN crew used a special four-wire phone line and satellite uplinks to transmit both audio and video pictures from the Iraqi capital. But in this era of instant global communications, as technology binds the world together, economics and market forces may pull in other directions. Moreover, fallible humans still shape the messages recorded and broadcast. Structures explores the mixed results of the new media systems, including changes in American broadcasting as the networks "downsize" their commitment to serious news and public affairs coverage. The interactions of the public good and the bottom line are considered.

In the second section, Face of the News, I explore the role of styles and personality in television. Magazines have distinct covers; newspapers use graphics and typefaces to alert readers to what is inside the rest of the edition. Television news also has its own distinct look in the morning, evening, and late at night—and I explore how the face of television is tied to its fortunes.

The third and principal section, Case Studies, offers specific examples of the media treatment of some defining topics of the late 1980s and early 1990s. Television news gets particular attention. Topics taken up include the coverage of AIDS; the media as moral police in political campaigns; race, class, and the coverage of crime (the Tawana Brawley and Central Park jogger cases); the "new godfather" John Gotti and why the cameras are married to the mob; the secret of rising above mere fame (how some men and women become candidates for Mount Rushmore); and the journalistic hazards of enlisting in the cold war. I raise and try to answer several questions about media performance, such as, Did the level of drug abuse go up in the 1980s, or only the level of news coverage?

What happens when terrorists seize hostages, *and* the network cameras? How are contemporary American images of the Japanese complicating the telling of the story of Japan Inc.? What changes occurred in White House press coverage when Ronald Reagan was succeeded by George Bush?

In the final section, Perestroika, I offer some suggestions for new media structures. Television news hardly ever discusses its own mistakes. It should. Television backs off when the news is about itself. It should not. Finally, I consider the consequences of the current implosion of the media, as print and electronic journalism begin to resemble each other.

Several of these reports, in different form, appeared in *New York* magazine, where I have been writing a regular column on the media, as well as longer articles, since 1985. I want to thank Edward Kosner, the editor and president of *New York*, for his advice and encouragement. He is the best conceptual editor I have encountered in over three decades of journalism—I also count him as a valued friend. A part of this work was done with the assistance of a number of students in the Department of Journalism at New York University. Among these helpers were Stephanie Acierno, Frank Accosta, Isabel Anacker, Christopher H. Bellitto, Tatjana Cukvas, A. Biddle Duke, Sharon Edelson, Gail Kellogg Kokubu, B. J. Kowalski, Adrian Marin, Rebecca Mead, Alan Mahony, Ellen McGrath, Paul Noglows, Katryna O'Neil, Anastasia Petryczka, Robert Silverman, Maggie Soares, Sylvia Steinert, Leslie-Jean Thornton, and Karen Wishod. I thank them all, as well as my colleagues in the department. In particular I am grateful for the support given my work by Professors Terri Brooks and David Rubin. I also thank Dean Duncan Rice and Associate Dean Ann Burton of the Graduate School of Arts and Sciences at NYU for their support in the preparation of this book.

All conclusions and opinions expressed here are my own, and I am solely responsible for them.

Structures

Television under *Glasnost*: Letterman Meets Lenin

1

On Wednesday, 15 March 1989, Soviet television-viewers gathered in front of their sets for the regular evening newscast of "Vremya" (Time), the chief television news program in the USSR. The plenum, or full meeting, of the Communist party's central committee was in Moscow to elect—or, more precisely, to approve—the official slate for the new Soviet People's Congress. The meeting would also hear something far less predictable: a speech by Mikhail Gorbachev on the deepening agricultural crisis in the Soviet Union. The 100 million viewers got more than they tuned in for. At 9:00 P.M., the blue-globe-and-red-star logo that announces "Vremya" flashed on screens throughout the USSR's eleven time zones (the program is taped in Moscow and retransmitted on the two national channels). The two anchors, a dark-haired man and a blonde woman, quickly introduced the session of the plenum itself. It was the first time cameras were allowed to cover the central committee. Gorbachev spoke . . . and spoke, past the usual 9:35 P.M. sign-off time for "Vremya," beyond the 10:00 P.M. interview scheduled with the great ballerina Maya Plisetskaya. After 11 P.M., "Vremya" ended its coverage of the speech (which Gorbachev had actually given earlier in the day) and tried its hand at some reporting. An interviewer asked Gorbachev, "Are you nervous about the outcome of the leadership ballot?" The Soviet leader paused. "Yes, one is always nervous." End of coverage.

Yes, the revolution will be televised. *Perestroika* and *glasnost* are topics discussed on all the Soviet television talk shows. Gorbachev speaks of revamping 60 years of agriculture policy by allowing farmers to "lease" land and pass on the titles to their children, which sounds very much like the return of private property. Soviet television reporters tentatively ask the leader "human" questions. Caught up in the excitement of the second Russian Revolution, American journalists in Moscow have begun to feel, as one reporter says, "a little like John Reed." But there was no discussion of Gorbachev's speech on the Soviet news. For a visitor from the United States, George Orwell remains a good guide to the unfolding events. For each tentative step forward by the state radio-TV committee toward more open discussion on the national-broadcast channels, the same authorities take a half step back—and sometimes a full step back. The voices of progress and reaction exist side by side, each claiming to represent the authentic will of the people.

Since Lenin, Soviet leaders have recognized the importance of the state's monopoly of mass communications. In the Brezhnev era (1964–82), Gostelradio, the state committee on television and radio, linked up the vast Soviet land mass. By the eighties, 86 percent of Soviet adults were telling researchers that television was their chief source of information. Yet many viewers were not pleased with what they saw. "Vremya" was regarded as something of a joke, with its boring lineup of official news, ribbon cuttings, and features on farm collectives. Even the stolid Brezhnev complained that the programs "do not give anything to either the mind or the heart." Leonid Zolotarevsky, one of the founding editors of "Vremya" and now a Gostelradio commentator, told me during an interview in his office that he used to let "months go by" without watching. Perhaps the low point for official news in the post-Stalin years was the coverage of the Chernobyl nuclear accident in April

1986. For three days, no news of the disaster came out of Moscow. Then came a five-sentence dispatch about "measures" (unspecified) being taken to "eliminate consequences" (also unspecified). According to Jonathan Sanders, then at Columbia University's Harriman Institute and now at CBS News, "Vremya" ran the Chernobyl story as its sixth or seventh item over the next few days. But in the United States, the "CBS Evening News" began with Chernobyl on six consecutive weekdays.

The Gorbachev regime has allowed changes in Soviet television, even if many are merely cosmetic. Graphics and logos have been freshened, and some anchors now read from TelePrompTers rather than hand-held clipboards. Cameras come in for close-ups, like the images of Gorbachev during his plenum appearance. Other changes are more substantive. The 1988 earthquake in Soviet Armenia received timely and extensive coverage, though Soviet TV did pay a price for pursuing Western-style human-interest stories. One earthquake victim who was eagerly offered up as a heroic "survivor" of weeks spent trapped under piles of rubble turned out to be an enterprising young man angling for some medical attention.

As in the United States, Soviet news-watchers tend to be older. And so Gostelradio has an Editorial Office for Youth Programming to create shows for new audiences in the *glasnost* era. Some of these programs do quite well, but none has the monopoly that makes "Vremya" the most-watched news program in the world. Weekday mornings, from 6:30 to 8:30 A.M., "120 Minutes" borrowed, at least to Western eyes, elements of the "Today" show, "Sesame Street," and MTV. On local Moscow TV, "Good Evening Moscow!" had more talk, news, and music videos. The monthly "Before and After Midnight," with smooth-talking thirtysomething host Vladimir Molchanov had a similar format, with an occasional Michael Jackson video. The most talked-about new program was "View," a late-Friday-night show aimed directly at the Pepsi generation in the Soviet Union. The hosts in the spring of 1989 were youthful; she was 30, he was 26; they dressed informally; and their writers seemed to be more influenced by the irreverent American television personality David Letterman than by the nominally revered Lenin. The program occasionally invited viewers' suggestions for a satiric, Letterman-like "museum of shoddy goods." On one Friday night, the museum included such displays as a cookie jar containing only scraps of paper (promises instead of performance), an empty coffee tin (more shortages), and an old rag that was supposed to represent hospital swaddling for newborn babies (a reference to the Soviet Union's high infant-mortality rates). At other times, "View" makes its points directly, without satire. One of its guests was historian Roy Medvedev, who until the Gorbachev openness was treated as a "nonperson" for keeping alive the issue of Stalin's crimes against the Soviet people. Now the terrible body count of Stalinist victims is openly argued in the Soviet media.

But all this surface openness is played out within strict confines. In 1989 Gostelradio gave over an entire hour on Sunday evenings to the program "Seven Days," to explore the week's issues in depth and to offer commentary. Many times the commentary, as Gostelradio people explain it, did not "coincide" with what the government's own position was. Moreover, the reprise of the week's news proved to be rather grim; in a typical week in 1990, the viewers saw images of ethnic turmoil, Lithuanian secession, earthquakes, miners' strikes, and other scenes of bad news. When these stories were all pulled together and presented one after another, "it added up to a terrible picture of Soviet life," one of the younger reporters at Gostelradio explained to me.

Learning to live with a free press can be a demanding experience. Soviet television people have developed a sort of Newspeak to explain what they are up to these days. The key terms are "hard news" and "soft news." Hard news is what officials are saying officially: the party line heard on "Vremya" and printed in the major papers like *Pravda* and *Izvestia*. Soft news is the feature segments, alternating with music videos and late-night skits. But even soft news is still official news, getting out the message that the state wants out. Soft features may dwell on quality-of-life issues: crime, grime, queues, bureaucratic incompetence. They may take up, in the official Newspeak, "the broadening of the sphere of commodity and money relations"—in translation: moves toward a market economy. In point of fact, then, the soft news is actually quite hard, and important. It is the news that really affects people, while hard news is the predictable boilerplate, not worth attending.

Recently, "Vremya" and Gostelradio have been making soft news—that is, real news. After Gorbachev came to power, he appointed his own man, Valentin Lazutkin, as Gostelradio chairman. In early 1989 Lazutkin named Eduard Sagalaev, who came out of the youth programming office, as editor-in-chief of "Vremya." Western journalists say the promotion must be envisioned in terms of the editor of *Rolling Stone* taking over at the *New York Times*. But the true power in Soviet television remains in the ideological section of the party politburo. Gostelradio reports to the section, as do all Soviet newspapers, magazines, record and music companies, and book publishers. The ideological section is responsible for the way the news, hard *and* soft, in all Soviet media, is treated. The new editor Sagalaev began his tenure cautiously, working to improve graphics, making the camera more assertive. Changes in content were still a way off, despite the new courage and inquisitiveness of many Soviet journalists. Authority still belonged to the party, and bolder moves will require a television system independent of the state. That can happen only when broadcasters get something like a lease on the TV "property" comparable to the lease Gorbachev is promising Soviet farmers. The audience was not holding its collective breath in anticipation.

A telling present-day illustration of how far *perestroika* and *glasnost* have come, and how far they still must go, occurred in

May 1990, when I returned to Moscow to look in on Gostelradio once again. A rising star of Soviet television, Sergei Medvedev (no relation to the historian), was showing his visitor around the offices of "Vremya." The 32-year-old Medvedev and Sergei Mormikto, 48, the "Vremya" supervising editor for the day, were trying to help their guest understand the chain of command at Gostelradio. In particular the conversation turned to Gostelradio's decision not to broadcast all the tumultuous events of the past May Day parade in Red Square. After the first official marchers from youth groups, labor unions, and party organizations had passed in review, some people in the so-called second wave demonstrations had jeered the Soviet leadership on the platfrom atop Lenin's mausoleum. The two men seemed to be knowing guides to these events. Medvedev has been making his reputation as a bright young broadcaster since the summer before, when his daily reports from the meetings of the Supreme Soviet (roughly, the parliament) were carried daily and—on occasion—live and unedited. Mormitko, a 22-year broadcast veteran, often takes reponsibility for the nightly "Vremya" story lineup, signing off on the selection and rotation of the stories.

Medvedev and Mormitko's conversation with their guest danced around the May Day decision, and a name kept coming up: one Nyetnashe. He apparently made the decision not to cover the second wave, and he kept the subsequent controversy off the air, while all of Moscow was talking about it. And what is Nyetnashe's first name and title? Laughter at the expense of the visitor. *Nyetnashe* means "not ours." While the staff may have wanted to keep broadcasting, the decision had been passed on from the newsroom to Gostelradio officials and others higher up—"not ours." "We are still part of the government," Mormitko explained, "and at present we have to reflect its policies. The decision was theirs, not ours." Nyetnashe may have carried the day on 1 May, but it was not clear to the "Vremya" staff that the collective Nyetnashe— the chiefs in the politburo—would make the same decision the next time. "There are different points of view among the ministers," Medvedev said, evenly.

Medvedev and his colleagues now have to contend with conservative forces among their viewers and within the party and government. For many, there was a sense that events were moving too fast. Discussing the May Day noncoverage with a Western visitor, a 40-year-old middle-level official of the Novosti press agency denounced the marchers, not Gostelradio. The second wave demonstrators, she said, had insulted the country. For her, and, it seemed, for many others in the Soviet television audience, it was an emotional matter, an issue much like flag burning for many Americans. The woman was upset by the demonstrators' boorish "Un-Soviet" behavior. Medvedev and other correspondents say that a "cooling down" has set in since the summer of 1989 and the time of official openness exemplified by coverage of the Supreme Soviet sessions. A Soviet silent majority, seeing the old tenets of society questioned, was worried that it no longer stands on any firm ground. It yearned for stability.

An increasingly beleaguered Gorbachev himself picked up on these tremors. In November 1990, the return to some of the bad old ways was signaled by Gorbachev's appointment of a conservative, Leonid P. Kravchenko, as the new director of Gostelradio. Under Kravchenko, Vremya in particular once again began sounding the tired themes about "provacateurs" and foreign "conspirators." Soviet liberals were reminded of the old Communist Party propaganda line that blamed economic shortcomings on Western plots.

Television news, then, has become a pressure point in Gorbachev's Soviet Union. When younger staff members like Medvedev sit around the Gostelradio commissary and weigh the future of "Vremya" and of television news in the Soviet Union, they know what they would like to see. They want an alternative to the official news, a kind of "people's TV" free of the state. Five or ten years from now, when new channels open up and cable television technology comes to the Soviet Union, Medvedev says, "I would like to be a part of it. I could be a commentator, and give my own point of view." He pauses a beat, and then adds, "I have one, you know."

Downsizing the News

2

At ABC News, President Roone Arledge calls it "reinventing the news." At CBS News, President Howard Stringer speaks of "streamlining the process." At NBC News, the phrase is "reevaluating the mission." Whatever the different buzzwords around the networks, the abiding concerns are the same. The ABC, CBS, and NBC news organizations are now recasting themselves—not, as in the past, because of the imperatives of journalism or technology or changing audience tastes, but because the networks' new owners demand it. The result was predictable: a news report of lowered aspirations.

When, in the summer of 1990, Iraqi forces invaded Kuwait, American television news organizations responded quickly to the developing crisis. Correspondents and camera crews were dispatched to the Middle East; the coverage was extensive, and viewing increased, as the audience for news responded. But there was a downside to the coverage. The deployment of these resources served to remind the careful viewer of TV news's corner cutting and its gaps in attention the rest of the time: the rich Middle East fare pointed up the skimpiness of regular news meals. Before the Gulf War began, the old-line broadcasters were guilty of doing what consumer watchdog groups discovered was happening on American supermarket shelves at the beginning of the 1990s. The makers of StarKist tuna, Knorr soup, Brim coffee, and other familiar brands had quietly reduced their product's weight or volume—without changing the container's size or lowering the price to reflect the reduction. General Foods, for example, began putting 11 1/2 ounces of coffee beans in the Brim can that had held 12 ounces. So, too, ABC, CBS, and NBC. Only CNN, the all-news cable network, seemed capable of giving full value from around the world.

It seems like only yesterday that the networks' evening newscasts were an anticipated part of life's routine. They came on at the same time each night and followed a comfortable format: Washington, foreign, Dow Jones, heartland, warm feature. Each had evolved from a fifties newsreel style (fifteen minutes held together by a narrator) through an increasingly ambitious news-headline service to contemporary, highly visual programs able to bring in stories live. By and large, viewers were pleased with what they saw. While ratings slipped in the eighties, the size of the evening-news audience was still impressive: 50 million Americans regularly watched the three national "evening papers" at the beginning of the 1980s.

Then each of the old-line networks was taken over in the mid-1980s by proprietors who briskly moved to control costs and cut back staff. Management experts arrived—the accountants from Coopers & Lybrand at CBS, the consultants of McKinsey & Company at NBC. At ABC, Arledge did not wait to be pushed, and began his planning without benefit of consultants at his elbows. But the results at ABC were not much different from what the time-and-motion studies produced at CBS and NBC. No one at ABC, CBS, or NBC seriously debates whether network news operations should be cost-conscious. The journalists have acquiesced to the new owners' notion that news programs must pay their own way rather than be supported by profits generated by the entertainment schedule. In "the old days" of broadcasting, just a generation ago, William S. Paley at CBS and David Sarnoff at NBC saw nothing amiss with taking from "Gunsmoke" and Johnny Carson in order to support their news organizations. Now the principle of profit from news exists, benign in the abstract, crippling in practice.

The attacks on expenses and the cutbacks in staff touched off labor-management strife unusual for broadcasting. In 1987 the newsroom union at ABC and CBS went on strike over the owners' intention to trim personnel without regard to seniority. Later there were bitter strikes at NBC, and again at CBS. The Reagan-Bush years made such anti-union activities relatively easy for managements. Broadcast executives found it harder to figure out how their leaner, more constricted organizations would gather and present the news. The year 1988, with the presidential elections and the Olympic Games, was good for the networks' business; but in subsequent years the healthy revenues and steady profit growth that were taken for granted a decade ago no longer automatically materialized. Some change in network news was no doubt inevitable, dictated by the increasing sophistication and popularity of local newscasts, the competition from cable television and from independent stations, economic recession and the softening advertising market, and the new auditors of broadcast-company stocks on Wall Street. Above all, there was the unsentimental expectations of the new owners. The three networks' inconclusive news rivalries also added to the feeling that change was inevitable. Each network usually had one financially successful news program: ABC's one-topic program "Nightline," CBS's perennial magazine show, "60 Minutes," and, until late 1989, NBC's "Today" show in the mornings. Meanwhile, at CNN, the 24-hour all-news cable network had a winning "program" around the clock.

The first decisive break with the past developed out of what began in 1986 as a pleasant tour of the CBS European bureaus by CBS's proprietor, Laurence Tisch, and his president for news, Howard Stringer. CBS News had a budget for 1987 of around $290 million. By the time Tisch and Stringer arrived in Paris, Tisch did not need the back of a Tour d'Argent menu to calculate that a lot of his money was being spent, essentially, for the 30 minutes of the "CBS Evening News with Dan Rather." Tisch took note of the "swollen" London bureau, the "redundant" crew based in Rome, and—back in New York—the atelier of 11 artists employed to produce graphic materials for the "Evening News." A stranger to journalism for the first 63 of his 64 years, Tisch listened as correspondents voiced the correspondents' timeless complaints about getting on the Rather program only twice a month. The owner's response was businesslike: why not do the Rather program with fewer people? The American visitors were also intrigued by European news-gathering procedures. Many stations rely on syndicated tape packages, which are broadcast newsreel-style. Once back home, CBS management began "Europeanizing" its operations, closing news bureaus in Bangkok, Warsaw, and Seattle and laying off 200 people, including 20 on-air correspondents, out of the news staff of 1,200. Other operating savings reduced the 1987 budget by up to $30 million. "Streamlining is painful," Stringer acknowledged. Among the most pained was Rather, who saw the cuts as directly affecting CBS's ability to gather the news.

Streamlining meant fewer newsroom employees and more videotape packages. When the "CBS Evening News" carried a story on the "Ivan the Terrible" trial in Jerusalem, an Israeli pool camera recorded the courtroom confrontation between John Demjanjuk, accused of being a sadistic Treblinka guard, and Eliyahu Rosenberg, a Treblinka survivor. Pooled picture arrangements are often necessary at trials; in this case CBS did not even use a report from outside the courtroom from its local correspondent. Instead, the tape of the scene was transmitted directly to New York, where Rather provided the narration. "No CBS film crew at $250,000 a year, no high-priced [CBS Tel Aviv correspondent] Bob Simon, only the transmission charge," mused a CBS producer in Washington. "That's how we do our business now."

Stringer put a more upbeat spin on these developments. He did not "dismantle" CBS's news-gathering operation—"We still have twenty bureaus"—or turn the "Evening News" into the "domain of stars sitting in Washington and New York." For one thing, that would look too much like local TV, where "generic" anchors do narrations. That would mean CBS was forfeiting its global reach, further blurring differences between local and network newscasts. The plan was to emphasize "analytical reporting"—thereby reducing the expensive coverage of a lot of breaking news. By definition, if television news is not based on being first with exclusive images, then it must be reflective. Besides cutting costs, the newfound love for an analytical approach acknowledges the network's inability to compete for spot news: the local news broadcasts go on first, and CNN is on 24 hours a day.

Initially, ABC had the least to lose in any major remaking of its programs. In the middle 1980s, its evening news program consistently trailed the competition's. You can not fall out of the basement, television wisdom holds, and so "World News Tonight" was moved to 6:30 in the New York market, coming on earlier than its opposition and, not so incidentally, opening up the 7:00 P.M. time period for another program, the enormously profitable game show "Jeopardy!" "World News Tonight" also borrowed a page from *People* magazine, introducing a "Person of the Week" every Friday night. But these were still cosmetic changes. Roone Arledge assembled his senior executives and producers at a corporate retreat to consider what ABC could be like if it were to try and reinvent itself. Though ABC has much the same news organization, technology, and corporate pressures as CBS, Arledge and his planners came out with different solutions. After the meeting, Av Westin, one of the executives present and then overseer of the ABC News show "20/20," was inspired to put his thoughts on paper. Westin called his 18-page document "Days of Penury, Days of Affuence." The penurious times were the sixties, when Westin was a young producer and when ABC News, with few resources, had to anticipate stories and act prudently. By contrast, in the days of affluence, a period that seemed to commence with Roone Arledge's arrival, Westin argued that sensible journalism often yielded to big spending. Westin sent his ideas to Arledge, to other ABC executives, and to Capital Cities/ABC chairman Tom Murphy and president Daniel Burke. Photocopies also ended up in the hands of reporters. Westin says the document was written as a magazine article; some of his critics within ABC say it was meant to be Westin's application for Arledge's job. If that was the intention, it did not work: Westin was removed from his posts at ABC.

Westin is a thoughtful, experienced television journalist. His proposals point to where the new ABC News is heading (one of management's allegations against him was that he had gathered others' views under his name). Westin and Arledge agreed, for example, that it may not make sense for ABC to keep a crew in Chicago if the local ABC-owned station can cover the spot news or if a cheaper, nonunion bureau can be set up in St. Louis. But the new "World News Tonight" reflected more and more Arledge's own personality-oriented news values, as well as budget-induced staff cuts. Arledge wanted to get certain ABC people on the air more often: for example, Pierre Salinger, the former White House press secretary in the Kennedy administration. These correspondents would be assisted by off-air talent, legmen and legwomen modeled on the old-time newspaper reporters at police headquarters, who phoned in the raw material for stories to their city desks ("Hello, sweetheart, gimme rewrite"). In television terms, these unseen, presumably younger, certainly less well paid, hands would furnish videotape as well as copy for the on-air correspondents. Sometimes they might appear on the newscast themselves. ABC would be creating a class system, consisting of first-magnitude stars and "others." Again, as with CBS, the midlevel people would disappear. All this would happen incrementally. While the future may not go back to the days of penury, it will nevertheless be a little like the past. "If you want to know what 'World News Tonight' will look like in the 1990s," one member of the retreat group told me, "think of the old Walter Cronkite news, with its resident company of reporters: Dan Rather at the White House, Roger Mudd from Capitol Hill, each appearing every night."

NBC News used to project a picture of health and confidence. The "NBC Nightly News" gained a perceptible lift from NBC's entertainment schedule, as well as from its own good work. Because of its successes, NBC once felt freer to go after a higher circulation. In the old days, the "Today" show spent over $2 million to be a highly visible presence in Australia during an America's Cup competition. NBC's new president, the GE man Robert Wright, had a new approach. He approved a 15-minute business show for the early morning lineup, and a Sunday edition of "Today." The added time was intended to "amortize" news costs in the currently desired fashion. NBC also began looking over its shoulder at the competition from local stations. NBC commissioned "The News Mission Study" to explore viewer attitudes about network news versus local news. The study produced the unsurprising conclusion that viewers want local newscasts to give local news and network newscasts to give national and international news. More pointedly, though, the study found that viewers perceive network journalists to be knowledgeable and professional—and look for those qualities when they turn on the news. NBC executives take that finding as justification for continuing to show off correspondents.

NBC also commissioned a McKinsey report. McKinsey consultant teams visited domestic bureaus; they also made the circuit of European bureaus, looked into non-NBC sources for videotape packages, and considered alternate ways to cover developing news—for example, by relying more on coverage by affiliates. The "NBC Nightly News" started a "Special Segment" with stories that sometimes ran for four minutes. The "Nightly News" also pushed Tom Brokaw into more live interviews of newsmakers at the scene of the story. As NBC increased the length of its stories and expanded

Brokaw's interview role, the number of spot-news stories and bureau reports was reduced. The new "NBC Nightly News" began to look like some other familiar television programs: Ted Koppel's "Nightline" and Robert MacNeil and Jim Lehrer's "NewsHour" on PBS (both modestly budgeted by network television standards).

One model for the network news of the middle and late 1990s could be the worst-case possibility: no network news at all. NBC was worried enough about this potential development to ask viewers what they would think if the NBC network became merely the news suppliers for the local newscasts. The audience was decisive: It did not like this idea at all. The question was not completely off the wall, viewed from the owners' self-interested perspective. Of the three old-line networks, only one usually makes a profit from its operations in any given year. Of course, neither of the parent corporate entities of the other two actually loses money. Profits from their stations in New York, Chicago, Los Angeles, and other big cities, and from their nonbroadcast operations, more than make up for network-operation losses. For example, in 1986, the first full year of operation for Capital Cities/ABC, the company reported a net income of $447.7 million, although the ABC network was an estimated $50 million in the red.

Rather than disappearing, the network newscasts of the near future will reflect the downsized news organizations that are putting them together—news operations with fewer bureaus and correspondents, more syndicated packages, and greater reliance on the braceros, the low-visibility harvesters of the news crop. The stars will still shine. The networks will at last achieve a certain "product" differentiation as each tries to find a cheaper, winning formula. Most likely, the ratings leader will still have a polished look, producing a sparkling miniature of the "days-of-affluence" shows that the networks trained viewers to appreciate in the seventies. The trailing networks' newscasts, on the other hand, will stir even dimmer memories—of fifties newsreel-style news.

Behind the Peacock Throne

3

The best stars and the brightest brass of NBC are meeting in Washington with the owners and managers of their affiliates, the 208 stations that make up the NBC network. Happy talk is heard everywhere, huge signs on the stage of the National Theater where the sessions are being held present more slogans than in a new socialist country. "NBC: Vision for the '90s" (a change from the "Proud as a Peacock" line that played upon the NBC symbol) . . . "Wherever News Breaks, Whatever It Takes." But the real message NBC was trying to get across in the early summer of 1990 was that of family, specifically the NBC family and how much everyone loves and needs each other during these uncertain times. Robert Wright, the General Electric career manager charged with running NBC since GE bought the network in 1986, praised the network-affiliate "partnership" and their "commitment to each other" through a trying period of wavering audiences and competitive challenges. Michael Gartner, the former newspaper publisher then in charge of NBC News, talked up "our growing family"; Jane Pauley was joining Tom Brokaw on the "NBC Nightly News"; Joe Garagiola was moving to the "Today" show couch alongside Bryant Gumbel and Deborah Norville; Maria Shriver would anchor a new prime-time series aimed at luring a younger audience to the NBC hearth. Dick Ebersole, head of NBC Sports, was adding to the NBC family as well, bringing NBA basketball and Notre Dame football to the schedule. Warmth fairly flowed from the stage. Jane remembered how she met her future husband at Tom's house, and Joe hugged Bryant, and Deborah smiled a perfect smile. The newest Schwarzenegger, Maria reported, weighed in at nine pounds; Dick said his wife, the actress Susan Saint James, was momentarily expecting their third child.

We all come home to family when we are in trouble. The Brokaw "Nightly News" had slipped from first to third in the ratings behind ABC and CBS; the "Today" show had gone into free fall after the network brass fumbled the elevation of Norville, and lost the morning services of Pauley in the bargain. The NBC primetime entertainment schedule looked shaky: after five years of supremacy, NBC must fend off an innovative ABC—the locale of "Twin Peaks"—and the upstart Fox network, home of the Simpson cartoon family. Understandably, some of the affiliates were skeptical of all the family talk. When GE took over NBC, recalls a network veteran present at the time, "there was an outsiders' buttoned-down arrogance about everything connected with broadcasting." Then, GE complained that the affiliates received too much compensation for their network contracts and that network talents were paid too much. "Now," says the former NBC man, "management is protesting love for its stations and the importance of its stars." Nostalgia has set in for "the Tinker years"—the time a decade ago when the affable Grant Tinker, an executive experienced in the ways of television and show business, was running NBC for RCA, the founding owners.

In its defense, the "new" NBC argued that the NBC entertainment schedule was still number 1, that management could make the transition, in Wright's words, "from the good old days to the good new days," and that in any case all three of the old-line networks were suffering audience defections. An oversize graphic flashed on the screen at the affiliates meeting charted the straight-line plunge in the three-network share of viewers—from

90 percent in 1980 (nine out of ten homes then watching television were tuned to ABC, CBS, or NBC) to a 63 share in 1990. Worse, for the 1990 summer rerun season, the share figure dropped into the 50s. Other charts testified to dramatic changes in the television business over the past decade: the number of homes with cable had gone from one in five in 1980 to more than one in two in 1990; VCR ownership had grown from practically zero to 65 percent; and independent TV stations had increased in number from 120 in 1981 to over 400 by 1990.

Beyond these industry-wide changes, however, NBC management in the post-RCA era had made its own contributions to the incredible shrinking universe. NBC decision making seemed improvised, and increasingly desperate. In the first six months of 1990 the "Today" show changed its executive producers as well as its cast; there seemed to be *two* people for every on-air job. Ebersole, who arrived in July 1989 to supervise the program (in addition to his demanding duties at NBC Sports), took the blame for the Norville-Pauley fiasco and was no longer involved with "Today." In May, a week before the affiliates' meetings, the reliable Bill Wheatley, executive producer of the "Nightly News," was let go, as if to propitiate the gods of the stations. Other human sacrifices were discussed at the same time—supposedly, Norville's—with the decision to hold off so that the network did not appear to its affiliates to be in greater chaos than they imagined.

All roads at NBC lead back to Fairfield—GE headquarters in exurban Connecticut. GE chairman John Welch presides in Fairfield. There, at the "officer's mess," as the corporate dining room is known, executives share their opinions about the world and NBC. The top managers like their NBC perks—the corporate jets flew off to Paris early in June for the French Open, broadcast by NBC Sports. GE executives do not hesitate to call NBC shots: Fairfield is where the Deborah Norville story first began, when someone said, in effect, "I like that girl; let's see more of her."

Lawrence Grossman, who was president of NBC News when GE took over, is a bit more charitable. "GE is very good at buying and selling companies," he says. "They had less interest in the quality of what was being broadcast." Grossman says he opposed certain GE proposals to "widen" the appeal of NBC News: specifically, the new owners' desires to put personalities like Geraldo Rivera and Morton Downey, Jr., on NBC. Grossman in 1987 also resisted a GE-inspired "simulation exercise" aimed at automatic reductions of NBC News's near $300-million yearly budget. He and his star anchor, Brokaw, had their differences. Buffeted from Wright above and newsroom people below, Grossman was gone after two years with GE. Wright, meanwhile, took as a prime assignment what GE called "broadening NBC's business base"—going beyond the company's traditional network operations into cable television and the new technologies. This hardly played well with the affiliates; from their point of view, partner NBC was proposing to go into business with competitive broadcast services in their own backyards. But Wright was worried about "dial market share." In the good old days, in most cities, NBC had one of the three or four channels available. Today, with 50- and 60-channel systems all around the country, NBC seeks more dial numbers. Under Wright, NBC acquired an interest in a sports channel, announced plans to offer some 1992 Olympic events on a pay-per-view basis, and started CBNC, a cable channel for business and consumer news (which also made room for the talk show host Morton Downey, Jr.).

While Wright had cable and satellites on his mind, Grossman's replacement, Michael Gartner, was asked to put the old technology of NBC News in order. Gartner had a law degree from NYU and impressive credentials as a top editor at the *Wall Street Journal* and later as president of the *Des Moines Register-Tribune*. He continued to write a column for the *Journal* editorial page and to maintain his residence in Iowa. He acknowledged that he had no television news background. But he knew the business side of media, and helped cut the NBC News budget to under $250 million. Independently wealthy from his newspaper executive days, Gartner came across as disdainful of others. He once suggested that the local broadcasters leave national and international coverage to the networks—at least that is what the affiliate station managers thought they heard him say. The affiliates also were angered at NBC's initial handling of the northern California earthquake in the fall of 1989. They even took a disliking to Gartner's trademark bow ties; when Gartner was introduced at the affiliates meeting, an actor in a suit of armor clanked onto the stage. The real Gartner then appeared, wearing a regimental tie, a belated signal of amnity.

In July 1989 Dick Ebersole became the supervising executive for "Today." GE men Welch and Wright, who supposedly abhorred executive layers in favor of lean management, were seen as interposing fresh bureaucracies in the news division. The "Today" show still was ahead of its closest opposition, "Good Morning America" on ABC, in the ratings, but the margin was shrinking. Because Ebersole was the new executive in charge, he had to do something "executivelike." Four decades of television news programming is testimony to the limited options available to such fixers at the top. The fixer can, in ascending order of cost, fire the producer, change the sets, or hire new talent (expensive if the old talent has a multiyear contract). "Today" already had decided to change producers, new graphics were in the works, Gumble was an untouchable. That left the show's newsreader, John Palmer, and its cohost, Jane Pauley.

Palmer was known as a "good soldier": he had 22 years of service at NBC. Pauley, too, did her work quietly, responded professionally to what was asked of her, and went home to her husband and children. She had an authentic family, not a videogenic assemblage. Once before she had put wider considerations ahead of personal ambition. In 1983, NBC had to choose between making Gumble or Pauley lead host of "Today"; although she had seniority, Pauley did not press her case because, she said, there had never been a black host at "Today." In 1989, approaching 40 and with almost 14 years on the morning show, Pauley was prepared to move on in her work. The ensuing well-publicized mishandling of her departure went beyond normal executive thick-headedness, and revealed a sexist and ageist mindset. By management's reckoning Pauley was middle-aged, telegenically speaking. Palmer, in his early fifties, was positively ancient. The elevation of Norville would enable NBC to banish signs of wrinkles or graying too early in the morning.

After Pauley's and Palmer's departure, the one volunteering to leave, the other pushed out, Norville won an expanded role. Two other women, Faith Daniels, 33, and Katherine Couric, also 33, were brought in as part of the growing family. Daniels had a Norville-like blonde-ambition look and was given the newsreader duties. Couric, based in Washington, had the perky young-woman-next-door look of the early Pauley. And there was a new—or rather, revived—white male, Joe Garagiola, at 64 old enough to be Palmer's uncle.

There is no science of programming; it is pure sleight of hand for anyone to wave computer printouts and claim knowledge of why certain personalities succeed once the red light on the television camera goes on, while others do not. Still, in the six months after the first reports of the Pauley-Norville story, some 600,000 viewers—a stunning 15 percent of the "Today" audience—tuned out of the program.

NBC management had its troubles at night as well. Tom Brokaw's "Nightly News" fell behind Peter Jennings's "World News Tonight" and Dan Rather's "CBS Evening News" in the ratings. All three network news programs found themselves talking to an increasingly quixotic audience. Serious news consumers knew that they no longer had to wait until the network shows came on during big news days. The major stories can always be found on CNN and, increasingly, on the local news that precedes the network programs. Brokaw was in Washington for the Bush-

Gorbachev summit in late May 1990, but so was Steve Handelsman of the NBC station group (a news organization serving the cities where NBC owns broadcast outlets, including New York, Chicago, and Washington). Handelsman reported the same story Brokaw was covering on the same NBC channels, but a full hour earlier.

Brokaw, Jennings, and Rather usually carry the same top stories; in the early evening the news is the news is the news. Their similarities expose an unpleasant little secret of news programming. The evening news form has, politely, reached its mature stage. After 40 years of development, there may be very little that can be changed or created without coming up against what one senior NBC correspondent calls "the wall"—the 22 minutes left for reporting after one subtracts time for the five commercial breaks in a half-hour news program. Efforts to shake up the structure mainly push at the edges, eliminating some elements, rearranging others, and rummaging among a finite range of already tested options.

Broadcast news needs to do something fresh. The risk taking on television is found more often in entertainment formats than on news programs. Perhaps it is too much to expect the news equivalent of a "Twin Peaks," with swaying traffic lights, rows of doughnuts, and the search for Laura Palmer's killer. If not "Twin Peaks," then a new "Nightline" will do. In the late 1970s, when Iranian militants seized the American embassy in Teheran, ABC started a late-night program to cover the story. The hostage crisis is long past, but "Nightline" remains, a simple idea: extended coverage of one event. The role of management is to make such innovation possible. Executives cannot order their staffs to be creative; they have to create the conditions where creativity flourishes, from the production assistants on up. Such conditions include strong staff morale, the feeling that someone is listening, and the conviction that good work will be rewarded.

The audience waits for that light bulb to go on over the heads of the GE men who run NBC.

Face of the News

The Vanishing Documentary

4

A few years ago, Burton Benjamin, a former CBS News executive who had a distinguished 27-year career as a television journalist, pronounced a kind of funeral oration for the traditional television documentary. The in-depth treatment of a single "serious" subject, he said, was being trampled in the networks' stampede to fast-paced ratings successes such as the magazine shows, "60 Minutes" and "20/20." Simultaneously, the traditions of caring journalism were being throttled by the same networks' announced intentions to make their businesses lean and mean. As a result, Benjamin said, the network documentary was an "endangered species," if not already DOA (dead on arrival).

Benjamin's requiem was delivered to a gathering at the Annenberg School of Communications at the University of Pennsylvania in February 1987. But the true burial of the traditional network documentary may actually have occured ten months later, when NBC News presented "Scared Sexless," with Connie Chung as chief correspondent. "Scared Sexless" took on such hot topics as AIDS and other sexually transmitted diseases, the singles scene, unwanted pregnancies, and sex education in the schools—all in *one* hour. It pantingly reported that open marriages were out and sexual fidelity in. And it did so in the company of such sex experts as Alan Alda and Goldie Hawn—both, as it happened, with just-released motion pictures to promote. A third expert was also on hand: Los Angeles Raiders football player Marcus Allen, described by Chung as being "as close to a single stud as one gets."

To round out this new-style "documentary," a female comic appeared every so often to tell tasteless jokes full of sexual innuendo. Chung herself, normally a journalist of taste and good judgment, performed some of her anchor duties while standing between two beds. The audience's response to this late-1980s-style "documentary" was equally perverse: the Neilsen survey numbers revealed that "Scared Sexless" achieved a 17.5 rating and a 30 share: almost one-third of all sets in use that Wednesday night were tuned to "Scared Sexless." It was the highest rated such NBC News program since NBC's "UFOs: Do You Believe?" in 1974. Less than a week after "Scared Sexless," the then-president of NBC News, Lawrence Grossman, announced that Chung would anchor two other programs, one on stress, and another on the "Aging of America." In addition, Maria Shriver would examine "Women Behind Bars." More traditionally, Tom Brokaw was assigned to programs on the homeless and on Islam.

Is the old-style documentary dead? NBC no longer calls these programs by that old designation, a name so redolent of the 1950s, of earnestly exhaustive journalism, and of traditional topics like migrant workers, hunger, or race relations. "Scared Sexless" was known as an "NBC News Report on America." Sometimes, such programs are called, simply, "NBC News Hours"—anything but "documentaries." And not just NBC is running away from the documentary form in word and deed. The other two old-line networks take a similar stand. "The word 'documentary' is pejorative," said Av Westin, then a senior executive at ABC News. "It sounds too much like a long trek through TV-land, a dry approach to a dull subject." Westin, a veteran journalist with a long record characterized by taste and good judgment, used to run "20/20"; then he became ABC News's vice-president in charge of "long-form specials" (Why say the one word "documentary" when three euphemistic words can be used?). Westin worked for ABC on plans for "one-theme magazines"—shows that break down single subjects into 15- to 18-minute components each with a storylike beginning, middle, and end: in effect, three one-act plays rather than one three-act play.

But perhaps the purest expression of the new style can be found at CBS News, home of some of the most memorable of the old documentaries. CBS's major long-form push for the 1990s is "48 Hours," which can best be described as an "antidocumentary." The traditional documentary ideal involved extensive background research and hours and hours of filming. Then came high concentration produced by means of careful editing: one person or a small group of persons pared down the raw materials to achieve a unitary vision, that is, an edited document. On "48 Hours," however, CBS parachutes down on a topic with a small army of reporters, producers, and camera crews. These troops swarm all over the story for two days and then present their results as "this-just-in" news: "48 Hours" goes to the mean New York City streets where the cocaine derivative crack is sold; "48 Hours" visits glitzy Las Vegas; "48 Hours" walks the wards and operating rooms of a Dallas hospital. The program is the opposite of a documentary: it is all you-are-there reality, with no editorial point of view. Again, though, viewers seemed to like CBS's antidocumentary form, just as they liked NBC's "Scared Sexless." The broadcast of "48 Hours on Crack Street" became the highest-rated CBS News special of the 1980s.

To hear network executives tell it, the blame—or credit—for these changes in public affairs television belongs to the audience. Blood, sex, violence, and money, we know, have always sold at the box office, at least since the age of Sophocles. But something else seems to be going on today. Contemporary viewers expect closure: a thesis, complicating action, and then a resolution, all in

10 or 12 minutes. That is the way television entertainment shows work. The public, according to this view, is now video educated. Too many of the old-style documentaries, Av Westin explains, "expected the viewer to wait around for a payoff until the last minutes, with two talking heads." In fact, the changing nature of the television documentary has less to do with the alleged mindlessness of the public than it does with radical shifts in the thinking taking place at the three old-line networks. It is the networks' new proprietors who are impatient for "payoffs." The old documentary form clings to life at the fringes of the networks' schedules; it also flourishes on public broadcasting, on cable television, and on other competitors of the Big Three. Classic documentaries are not dead; they have merely been displaced, and the story of their migration tells a great deal about the state of television today.

The old television documentary had its roots in the work of many talents. The tradition includes the classic theatrical films of Robert Flaherty, John Grierson, and Pare Lorentz. Journalistic newsreels, such as "The March of Time" series from Time Inc. and the "Why We Fight" series of World War II troop films, which engaged highly original directors such as Frank Capra, also contributed to the tradition. By the early 1960s, television had already made a substantial contribution to the documentary form and, as Burton Benjamin said, was about to enter its putative "golden age." Edward R. Murrow and Fred Friendly had produced the "CBS Reports" series. Benjamin himself had worked on "The Twentieth Century" series and Irving Gitlin was responsible for the early NBC "White Paper" programs. Filmmakers such as Robert Drew and Richard Leacock were involved at ABC News, where they experimented with hand-held cameras and cinema verité techniques. Within the space of a few weeks during one broadcast season, CBS did "Harvest of Shame," about migrant workers' conditions; NBC analyzed "The U-2 Affair" (a United States spy plane had been shot down over the Soviet Union); and Drew looked at American involvement in Latin America ("Yanqui, No!"). In 1963 NBC offered "The Negro Revolution," which was broadcast for three and a half hours on one night. In 1966 CBS broadcast 22 documentaries, while ABC and NBC each broadcast 15. In 1986, 20 years later, the combined *three-network* production of documentaries had declined to 14.

As just about everyone is tired of hearing by now, the 1960s were different from the 1980s. Then, the country was at war, in Vietnam and at home: Negroes became angry blacks, students became vocal protesters, gays began to come out of the closet, and women became feminists. Network television documentaries reflected those tumultuous times and social movements, just as television has mirrored the more privatistic concerns of recent years. Naturally, there was televised fluff then as well as now. On the same late fall evening in 1966 that NBC was examining "The Battle for Asia-Thailand: The New Front," the same network was also offering "It's a Dog's World," a special broadcast narrated by the actor Lorne Greene, exploring the "relationship of man and dog through the ages." But by 1986 the balance of subjects had clearly shifted from the political to the personal. At NBC, for example, that year's four major documentaries—NBC still called two of them "White Papers"—covered AIDS, Japan's economic threat to the United States, divorce in America, and the crack menace.

As the country appeared to be retreating from the big political topics, television more and more abandoned the old long-form style of presentation. The admired success of the 1970s and 1980s was not the NBC "White Papers" or "CBS Reports"; it was the CBS magazine show "60 Minutes." Year after year, "60 Minutes" earned millions of dollars for CBS—as much as $70 million in some years, according to its outspoken, energetic executive producer, Don Hewitt. The networks rushed to find more such magazine hits; "20/20" was created at ABC and "West 57th" at CBS, while NBC experimented with a variety of formats, all failures to date.

Interestingly, NBC tinkered with the idea of "90-Minutes," a Sunday night rival to Hewitt's show. The combined forces of NBC News and the NBC Entertainment and Sports divisions were to be assembled in order to create what was described as "a free-form magazine with something of a variety show flavor." Ventures like "90 Minutes"—if they do make it to the air on a regular basis—suggest that the documentary form has devolved into a kind of infotainment, signalling the passage from the golden age to the time of fool's gold.

No institution can remain static over the years. Art forms change, so do building designs, automobile shapes, newspaper and magazine graphics. Today there are double the sources of broadcast news and information that there were 20 years ago. While there are fewer documentaries in the classic style, many of the old documentary themes are being covered by programs such as "Nightline" and the "Today" show; talk show hosts such as Oprah Winfrey and Phil Donohue take up traditional "documentary" themes, as well. Not everyone regards these changes as signs of progress. The veteran journalist and documentary maker Reuven Frank has been involved with television news since its infancy. He joined NBC News in 1950 and served as its president during the 1960s, perhaps television's most formative years. He offers three telling points about the state of informational programming today. First, Frank argues, "there is no documentary that can be produced in five minutes." While the technology is better today than 20 years ago, what matters is the way the subject is explored, and the time devoted to it. Second, in magazine shows today, "too often the emphasis is on the reporter rather than the piece being reported. That may make for good television, but not good journalism." Third, "the important thing is getting time on the network—that's what is hard."

This last is the dirty little secret of serious informational programming. Typically, the networks have hidden documentaries and news specials on their schedules. In Benjamin's words, several of the programs he worked so hard on in his years at CBS "wound up opposite the Oscars, the Emmies, Miss America, or on Christmas Night." The fine documentary work of Pamela Hill and Helen Whitney, two accomplished producers at ABC during the 1980s, might just as well have been available only on videocassette in stores. Whitney's much-praised study of mental illness, "They Have Souls, Too," appeared on a Friday night in late June 1987, at the start of a pleasant summer weekend, a time when viewers were not too likely to be looking forward to watching serious treatments of social concerns. The broadcasters' bad habit of giving *all* public affairs programs poor time slots persists, and so the gaudy new documentary forms do only marginally better than the old-style documentaries. NBC offered "Scared Sexless" on the night before New Year's Eve; CBS's "48 Hours" was given a time period opposite the top-rated "Bill Cosby Show" on NBC; in the fall of 1990, "48 Hours" was shifted to Saturday nights, again not a time when the audience is likely to want to think about matters of public policy.

The "networks" both Frank and Benjamin had in mind were ABC, CBS, and NBC. But as more and more viewers have come to recognize, the classic documentary form can now be found elsewhere, on public television stations and on cable systems. Reruns of Benjamin's own memorable series, "The Twentieth Century," with a forever young Walter Cronkite as host, play regularly on the Arts and Entertainment network on cable. WTBS, the Atlanta superstation created by Ted Turner, has offered the programs of Jacques Cousteau, the Audubon Society, and the National Geographic Society—precisely the kind of mature documentary that used to run frequently on the old-line networks. On the Public Broadcasting Service, the "Frontline" series commands a season-long one-hour time period. When the country marked the 200th anniversary of the U.S. Constitution in 1986, PBS presented Bill Moyers's excellent ten-part series, a reasoned consideration of the founding document. Moyers also did a three-part documentary series for PBS on "God and Politics," a theme that resonates with the old-form documentary. Moyers has not reverentially treated the form as if it were preserved under glass (like the U.S. Constitution itself). Rather, he has worked in the style of the old documentary without an excess of homage. When Moyers offered "The Secret Government . . . The Constitution in Crisis," he described it as a "personal essay." The program used a music video by Jackson Browne to introduce the rest of the (properly grave) proceedings.

Burton Benjamin died in 1989. Before his death, his discouraged tone modulated a bit. Programs like "48 Hours," he allowed, should be treated as good news. Or rather, "the idea of any factual TV, particularly long-form shows, getting on the air should be welcomed." No one can disagree with the proposition that what is done with the time is what really counts, whatever the name the program goes by. Unfortunately, a kind of class-mass split has developed in television. "Serious" informational programs, willing to call themselves documentaries, are gravitating away from the networks and prime time and are being seen in places and times that all but guarantee small, elite audiences. Meanwhile, punchy infotainment specials rise to the top of the old-line networks' schedules, where large audiences are normally on hand. It is as if two societies, and two sources of public discourse, have come into being in the country. Elites tune to an information-rich world; others have an information-poor diet. When that happens in a democratic society, a lot more than a program form becomes endangered.

Anchor War

5

"I know a lot of people think I've got the CBS eye tattooed on my ass," Dan Rather says, conceding his public image as a tough, hard-charging telejournalist. Yet during his workday, as he prepares for the "CBS Evening News," Rather frequently slips out the back door of the CBS Broadcast Center in New York City to the playground of a city housing project across West Fifty-sixth Street; from a bench, he takes the air, contemplating life, as immobile as one of the park winos. The real Dan Rather, he says, "simply loves the news."

A few clicks of the dial away from Rather, ABC's "World News Tonight" presents the modish, immaculately groomed Peter Jennings, the very image of the diplomatic correspondent with his English-cut suits and his mid-Atlantic diction. Off-camera, however, Jennings is tieless, hustling on the phone for stories, dragging on one of the scores of cigarettes he smokes daily, his voice revved up to talk-radio speed. He says he sometimes gets so emotional about stories that he once considered quitting ABC "to work for the refugees." His wife, Kati Marton (the third Mrs. Jennings), says the austere man on the screen is not the man she sees at home.

On "NBC Nightly News," Tom Brokaw looks just like another pretty face on local news in, say, San Jose or Phoenix. Around the NBC newsroom at 30 Rockefeller Plaza, however, a co-worker rechristened Brokaw "Duncan the Wonder Horse" in tribute to his prodigious work habits. In his office, Brokaw squeezes hand-exercise grips to fight down his tensions; privately, Brokaw is the one with the tattoo, the confrontational style. "I am formed," Brokaw says, in what might be considered a reference to one or possibly both of his rivals, "I don't reinvent myself every night."

Who says the camera does not lie?

The common perception is that what we see is what we get, that we know our anchormen, with their instantly recognizable faces, that we can call them by their first names: Dan, Peter, Tom. Each weeknight they come into millions of American households to deliver the news, familiar guests at our hearth: three white, prosperous, middle-aged males—Rather just past 60 in 1990, Jennings in his mid-50s, Brokaw, over 50. Each is highly qualified for his work. Even their programs are outwardly similar. After time for commercials is subtracted, each has 22 minutes of stories and the same general rotation of the news: Washington (White House and Congress), war zones (South Africa and the Middle East), American heartland (tornadoes, drought, farm foreclosures, 30-car pileups on California highways), and human or animal interest (the boy who fell through the ice, the baby born to the brain-dead mom, Bambi's mother and the three lost whales).

These rhetorical models have apparently grown so much alike that the viewing public itself gives them almost identical attention. The biggest news about the evening news at the beginning of the 1990s was that the holy writ of the Nielsen ratings showed that Rather, Jennings, and Brokaw each commanded an audience of about 13 million people, give or take a million. Looking at Dan, Peter, and Tom and their three evening broadcasts, it is possible to conclude, with apologies to Gertrude Stein, that the news is the news is the news. Possible, but wrong. To the alerted eye, Dan, Peter, and Tom, and their programs, are distinct from one another, as distinct as their on-air personae are from the men playing the anchor's role. What we get is not what we see, but something far more intriguing. The audience, subconsciously, knows this truth. Viewers have read the implicit iconography of the evening news and aligned themselves in accordance with their understanding of the subtext of each man and his program. The proof can be found in the ratings books: demographics never lie.

The iconographic Dan, of course, is country & western, appealing to an older, idealized America of the imagination. Peter is urban, projecting an image with which a more youthful market can identify. Tom positions himself somewhere in between, in the middle, as an avatar of suburban values. Together they constitute a three-way mirror of America that tells us where the country is today: see the tightened race among the triple demographies of the news. They also tell us where the country is heading tomorrow, as the weight of viewer numbers shifts toward one or another end of the scale.

Television news people pay lip service to Edward R. Murrow as their Founding Father. He is honored for his wartime radio broadcasts ("This . . . is . . . London") and his gritty CBS special reports and documentaries. They "don't make 'em anymore" like the program that took on Senator Joe McCarthy or like "Harvest of Shame," the documentary that alerted comfortable viewers to the plight of migrant workers. As we saw in the previous chapter, they rarely make them at all; "60 Minutes," "20/20," and the other current TV magazine shows normally offer more infotainment than exposé or social criticism. The network evening news is where the action is now, both for attracting big advertising dollars and for winning journalistic prestige. Curiously, Murrow never was a television news anchor and served only briefly, and poorly, as part of the CBS team during the national political conventions of the fifties and early sixties. There has been only one protoanchor, and his name is Walter Cronkite. The word *anchorman* was first applied to Cronkite at the 1952 conventions to connote the strongest performer, the man you would want running the final leg of a relay race.

Television news is divided into two historic periods: the years B.C., Before Cronkite, and the modern era. From the late sixties until he stepped aside, after a sharp shove in 1981, Cronkite presided over the top-rated network news program. He was, first of all, a consensus figure. He came not only from a simpler America, but also from the middle of the middle: he was born in 1916 in St. Joseph, Missouri, the son of a dentist. His circumstances were neither North nor South, East nor West, rich nor poor. Second, his journalistic training was in the objective mode of the wire services; Murrow hired him from United Press during the last great war. Yet Cronkite was not always Cronkite. He stumbled badly in the ratings at the 1960 and 1964 conventions; the early and mid-sixties belonged to NBC's Chet Huntley and David Brinkley. Huntley was a rugged native of the Big Sky country who rode in from a California television station and bore a certain physical resemblance to Murrow; Brinkley was from Back East, a Washington reporter who cast a cold eye on the game of politics. The Huntley-Brinkley bicoastal ticket won over the news audience, with Cronkite in the middle distance behind them. ABC, for all practical purposes, was nowhere; the Almost Broadcasting Company then fielded a weak, insubstantial news organization that attracted a minuscule audience. In 1965, desperate to compete and willing to try anything, ABC put forward a reporter named Peter Jennings as its evening news anchor. Though Jennings was only 26 at the time, he had already worked as an anchor in his native Canada. But the ABC audience, the ABC affiliates, the critics, and finally the ABC staff, all judged Jennings too young and too pretty for the job; after only two years he was busted back to the ranks of correspondents.

Cronkite versus Huntley-Brinkley was stage center, ABC the sideshow. Huntley-Brinkley, while not exactly a novelty act, did well enough as long as the news could be lightened up. But by the end of the 1960s, perhaps two million people had dialed out of NBC and switched to CBS, an unprecedented mass-media movement. The times demanded gravity. A lot of sixties' viewers were older folks: news watching, like voting in elections, has traditionally been a middle-aged activity, and CBS's prime-time entertainment schedule appealed to older, rural, and small-town audiences. This was the era of "The Beverly Hillbillies," "Green Acres," and "Hee Haw." But Cronkite himself also pulled in viewers, for this was also the time of Vietnam abroad and political assassination and racial insurrection at home. Hippies, yippies, strung-out veterans, blacks, rock & rollers, longhairs, gays, women's liberationists—all seemed to be shouting from the screen. Cronkite's modulated, "objective" demeanor calmed the fears of the mainly older, mainly white, mainly propertied viewing classes. When the Kennedys and King were killed, when the body bags came home from Vietnam, when the Chicago police rioted, and when the astronauts got stuck in orbit, it was Cronkite who anchored the nation's emotions in a way Huntley-Brinkley could never quite do. Cronkite had authority. When Cronkite returned from a visit to Vietnam in 1968 and expressed doubt about President Lyndon Johnson's war, Johnson concluded that having lost Cronkite, he had lost the country. The president therefore decided not to run for reelection.

The Cronkite consensus later began to come apart as the mass audience became younger, less middle class, and less white. The street children and urban rioters of the 1960s joined the settled, television-watching population of the 1970s. Fred Silverman, known at the time as the man with the golden gut—his own sensitivities were supposedly wired to contemporary tastes—was then in charge of ABC programming. His string of highly successful comedy shows and action entertainment, including "Laverne & Shirley," "Happy Days," and "Starsky and Hutch," brought younger viewers and especially women to ABC. The popularity of the ABC entertainment shows boosted ABC News. At the beginning of the 1970s, less than two-thirds of the network affiliates "cleared" the ABC evening news, that is, took the network's program and put it on the air; but by the end of the 1980s virtually all of the 200-plus affiliates were clearing ABC's program, putting it on as many "newsstands" as its CBS and NBC counterparts. By this time, too, the ABC product on the stands had begun to display a more contemporary look, with computer-generated graphics. Roone Arledge had taken over ABC News. At ABC Sports in the sixties and early seventies, Arledge had helped create the modern macho television sports era with instant replays, slo-mo, isolated cameras, and "honey shots" (three-second glimpses of attractive young women in the stands). He applied the new techniques to ABC News. Bankrolled by Silverman's dollars, Arledge spent money on the news as if it were . . . a sport. The sports division had paid hundreds of millions for the rights to broadcast professional football and the Olympic Games. What was a million more here or there for one more salary for one more news talent?

In the Nixon years, Dan Rather and Tom Brokaw were White House reporters for their networks, each earning no more than $125,000 a year. By 1979, they were both working in New York, Rather for "60 Minutes," Brokaw for "Today." Each was earning perhaps $300,000 when Arledge offered Rather $2 million a year (plus a role in everything at ABC News from anchoring the evening news to hiring and firing staff). Cronkite was earning half that. When Arledge could not sign Rather, he went after Brokaw, who also turned him down. To keep Rather's and Brokaw's loyalty, CBS and NBC had to play in Arledge's league. Rather got a pledge that the avuncular Cronkite would be hoisted as the CBS anchor, plus a ten-year contract that guaranteed him nearly $25 million. Later, his contract was sweetened; as the 1990s arrived, Rather was a $3 million-a-year man. Brokaw's Arledge-proof salary by then was around $1.8 million annually. "I've learned to live with the money, the celebrity, the criticism," Rather once told me. "They come with the territory."

For most of the mid-1980s, Rather and his "CBS Evening News" were number 1, the program the others tried to overtake. He was the front page of CBS News and, like Jennings and Brokaw, he was worth every penny of his salary. If his presence contributed to a positive shift of just one ratings point in the Nielsen numbers, from, say, a 10 to an 11, it meant as much as a $15 million gain in annual revenues from what CBS charged its advertisers. Rather does not make the first nights, the power meals, or the New York scene. He claims to be happiest lunching on a tuna-fish sandwich at the newsdesk in the Broadcast Center, sitting with the news staff, working on the story lineup. His daily prayer is, he says, "God, give me one more day at my work." Some of this, of course, is the kind of log cabinizing that politicians habitually do: self-serving stories showcasing their modest beginnings, diligent work habits, and simple desires. Rather today is a sophisticated journalist who seems to be consciously gearing down his high-intensity persona. A good performer, he is careful not to appear too fast for the room he is working. Yet "the book" on Rather, to borrow a favorite Ratherism, does begin in hardscrabble East Texas. He remembers that depression-era kids like himself aspired, at most, to be high school football coaches or airline pilots (Rather's younger brother is a high school principal, and his sister is a high school teacher). Rather's critics accuse him of constantly redefining himself, pulling on or peeling off sweaters at a tremor in the ratings, changing the color of his hair from black to gray to black again (a charge Rather denies). "Who is that guy inside the suit anyway," asks a former CBS colleague, "the one running around here saying, 'I'm Dan Rather'?" Rather says he knows who he is: "I am a reporter who cares about people." In his autobiography, *The Camera Never Blinks*, he writes that his father, Irwin "Rags" Rather, was an oil pipeline worker—a ditchdigger—and his mother a waitress.

One of the long-standing indictments of network news, thunder from the left and the right, is the charge that the decision makers are an elite; they are, it is said, cut off from "the people," and hooked instead to their closed-circuit communications and their regular morning diets of the *New York Times*, the *Washington Post*, and the *Wall Street Journal* (more input from people just like them). The state-of-the-art facility deep inside the CBS Broadcast Center, where Rather and his producers determine the nightly play of stories, is called "the fishbowl." It can be held up as symbolic of the social isolation of the modern newsroom, as are the similar rooms at ABC and NBC 20 Manhattan streets away from CBS. In all three newsrooms, the conference tables look out on newsdesks and closed-circuit monitors and television screens, not on the "real world"—as many of the denizens of the bowl are the first to acknowledge. But Rather claims to have a different perspective. "If you've come from where I've come from," he says, "standing in a ditch, shovel in hand, working with your back, that's a never-to-be-forgotten experience. No matter how high you rise, you can never get away from those formative years." Then, leaning forward, he smiles. "You're thinking to yourself, 'There goes the bulls——part.' " The listener is wondering if Rather is fusing his life with Rags's, but then Rather adds, "As Henry Kissinger once said, 'And it has the added advantage of being true.' "

Populism with an intellectual face: not to put too fine a point on it, that is as good a description as there is of Dan Rather and the "CBS Evening News." The CBS broadcast is the People's Republic of Rather. Rather did not create this state of mind by himself. He had the help of Van Gordon Sauter, the president of CBS News during the formative years of the program in the mid-1980s. When the occasion demanded, Sauter could put up his own log cabins. He is also from Small Town, U.S.A.: Middletown, Ohio, no less. His father was a fireman, his mother a saleslady. He went to Ohio University, studied journalism at the University of Missouri, worked on papers in Detroit and Chicago. When Rather took over the "Evening News" in 1981, and the ratings sagged a bit, it was Sauter who figured out the problem. "Dan was doing the 'CBS Evening News' . . . with Walter Cronkite!" he remembered.

CBS coverage was still in the style of Cronkite's straightahead wire-service report; it was a newscast of printlike headlines, a lot of them from congressional hearings, told with pictures. Rather and Sauter began taking the "Evening News" out of Washington and into the countryside. They wanted stories specifically aimed for television, stories that were built around people and their emotions.

Part of this change was generational: the slaying of the father Cronkite and the older executives who had worked with him and shared his print background. Cronkite was in no hurry to leave, and the memory of the changes still rankles (asked for his opinion of contemporary CBS news programs in a *Washington Post* interview, Cronkite pointedly expressed admiration for the syndicated show "Entertainment Tonight"). The Rather-Sauter regime promoted producers whose sole experience was in television, who liked video, and who worked to achieve visual epiphanies or, in Sauter's phrase, "moments" in people's lives. But the change from Cronkite to Rather also involved the whole Reagan eighties gestalt. The post-Cronkite program was meant to be antigovernment and antipolitics; "Miller time" instead of congressional hearings time—"This broadcast's for you." This meant evocations of ordinary people's lives, and the community of feelings, rather than the parade of authority (including the old authority figure of the anchor). This change did not mean that the Rather news on CBS offered an upbeat, Reaganite "shining city on a hill" vision; nor did it broadcast the airhead fluff of local news. In the summer of 1986, when "CBS Evening News" reported that the USX company was shutting down mills and that the LTV corporation was going into Chapter 11, Rather quickly moved from the institutional report of "Big Steel in trouble" to the little people's story of how the closings were affecting one disabled worker, depriving him of medical benefits. "Someone loses his or her job," Rather observed at the time, "and I want to show what's being said and felt."

This marked the shift from Cronkite news to Rather news. But almost 70 years ago, well before there was television news, the philosopher George Herbert Mead looked at the newspapers of his day and suggested that there were two models of journalism: informational news based on fact (the Cronkite show) and story news intended to create an aesthetic experience and help people relate events to their own lives (the Rather show).

It is the 3:45 P.M. news meeting, and Peter Jennings is going through the "World News Tonight" lineup with seven producers and news editors, six men and one woman; their average age appears to be about 35, typical of a significant percentage of the audience for "World News Tonight." At this particular meeting, Bill Lord, at the time executive producer of WNT, was on vacation, and Jennings, who had been the sole anchor for the program since September 1983, was clearly running things. But even when the executive producer is on hand, Jennings (like Rather and Brokaw) still has the anchor's ultimate, though rarely—if ever—used, power: he can say, "I don't want to do that," and it is not done.

Jennings and his producers agree that the toughest workdays are those when there is too much news and those when there is not enough news. This day, in late July, is shaping up as one of the former; some pieces will have to be held, or given away (to ABC's morning show "Good Morning America," for example), or simply killed. Jennings is wired. The producers offer up stories, and he swings hard at them. NASA will be making available the taped transcripts of the *Challenger* crew's last moments—weeks, someone says, after agency officials said that no such tape existed. Another producer smells cover-up or, at the least, foul-up. Jennings worries: "Is it too ghoulish? I don't want to be ghoulish." Next the LTV steel plant in East Chicago is shutting down, but no one can quite place the location of the town. Jennings remembers. It is in Indiana, and was the hometown of the late Frank Reynolds—before Jennings ABC's great anchor hope of the post-Cronkite era. Reynolds provides a geographical reference point for the news staff.

Jennings wants to know, "How sick is Ella Fitzgerald? Do we have a piece ready?" The singer is resting comfortably in the hospital, but her illness involved her heart; an obituary should be put together and held in the bank of available stories. One producer pitches a yarn about a tiger supposedly loose in the wilds of Pennsylvania. "I can see the picture now," says Jennings. "A bunch of highway patrolmen, guns drawn, peering down the road." No sale. From Washington, the ABC News bureau is offering a story about congressional hearings on crack cocaine. Jennings makes a prediction: "Not a day will go by for the rest of the year without some politician wanting to get on the air with his statement about the need for a 'crackdown on crack.' " There is no dissent.

The rest of the meeting goes back and forth on what to do about two features, each one qualifying as light show-enders. Television likes to send the audience off to prime time, and to the advertisers' messages, with a pleasant emotional buzz (the news permitting). Jennings has to choose between the opening of the Karpov-Kasparov chess match in London, and the story of Mi Dori, the 14-year-old violin prodigy, whose remarkable concert with Leonard Bernstein made the front page of the *New York Times* that morning. The concert was two nights earlier, and no network crews were present. Still worse, the producers are groping to remember the name of the town near the Tanglewood festival. Someone points out that CBS and NBC read the *Times*, too. The decision is made to hold the chess piece.

The meeting over, Jennings places a call to Bernstein, rolls copy paper into his Olympia manual, picks up the phone ("Hello! Maestro! How very nice of you to talk to me") and proceeds to play catch-up on the story, just one more street reporter getting a fill-in from a news source. Later, Jennings puts in some work on his regular Friday-night feature, "Person of the Week," a personality-centered report intended to engage younger viewers who normally dial out the news as the weekend approaches.

"Person" tends to be upbeat, a tribute to national leaders. Through the first 17 weeks of the series, only one genuine bad person made the roster (Jackie Presser of the Teamsters Union). That night Jennings leads with the NASA tape, as do Brokaw and Rather. There is a straightforward piece from Washington on plans for a Gorbachev-Reagan summit; mostly the story offers stenographic reporting of the official positions. The East Chicago steel story is also aired, as is a Special Assignment segment on crack by reporter John Quinones. The visual style of this package comes right out of "Miami Vice"; the editing seems certain to have its greatest impact on what the market researchers call the "urban core" audience. One sequence shows viewers the equipment needed to get in on all the excitement: a Maxwell House coffee can, a tinfoil lid, a cigarette lighter, crack, and you. The whole package ends with a close-up image of an eight year old, the next crack user, we are to conclude (certainly, if he follows the ABC's of it all).

That night's program was not typical. Overall, the "World News Tonight" broadcasts consistently offer solid journalism. As the decade of the eighties came to a close, Jennings and "World News Tonight" gradually overtook Rather and Brokaw in the evening news ratings. Quality was being rewarded; content analyses showed that WNT usually did more foreign news than its rivals. Predictably, CBS did the fewest foreign pieces, and NBC's international-story content fell in the middle. The Jennings news reflected the Jennings strengths, and also his basic character, as distinct from his image. Jennings's vaguely Oxonian urbanity is acquired. Though no ditchdigger (his father was an executive of CBC, the Canadian Broadcasting Company), Jennings is a high school dropout. His real school has been the road. After his brief run on the evening news in the mid-1960s, Jennings worked abroad for ABC on and off for the next 15 years. He helped open the ABC office in Beirut, the first American television news bureau in the Arab world. He interviewed Arafat, covered Khomeini's return to Iran and Sadat's assassination. "Jennings owned the Arab story," according to his friend Av Westin, a veteran news executive. Some American Jewish groups used to claim that the Arab cause owned Jennings; but the charge is heard less and less now and was ill-founded in the first place.

ABC's rivals hold that Jennings is "too intellectual." Surely, no one would mistake WNT for the CBC News, much less *Le Monde*. But Jennings is sensitive to any accusations that the program is not sufficiently "American." His Canadian citizenship does not seem to bother his viewers; out of the 900 letters he received after ABC's Liberty Weekend coverage in 1986, he says that almost all of the writers complimented him and that only three complained about a non-American anchoring the broadcasts. Nevertheless, Jennings works hard cultivating American stories, just as hard as he works at his Mr. Cool image: "Precisely because I was out of the U.S. for so long, I didn't take anything for a given after I came back." It was Jennings who first suggested a regular series to be called "American Portrait" for WNT; Arledge took this basically leaden idea and turned it into the glittery "Person of the Week." The early Jennings had played James Darren to Sandra Dee: when ABC made him an anchor the first time, it was looking to attract, he acknowledges, "a Gidget-type audience." Abroad, Jennings filled out. After two failed marriages and the glamorous life of a correspondent prowling the world, he now follows a more settled routine with his third wife and their two children in a Manhattan apartment. He has circles under his eyes and a developing bald spot at the top of his head (not visible on camera). As Av Westin says, "The sharper edges of the image have been eroded . . . he's one of the folks now." The Americanization of Peter proceeded so well that respondents to a recent Gallup Poll ranked Jennings second only to the gone-but-not forgotten Cronkite in that most important of all anchor qualities, "believability."

A critic once angered Tom Brokaw by referring to his "button nose." Others have judged Brokaw and the "NBC Nightly News" to be "bland," "neutral," "objective." When I suggested to Brokaw that, after watching several weeks of all three news programs, a group of us had placed him in the middle between the emotional, populist Rather and the suave, establishment Jennings, Brokaw hardly paused before he said, "I'll take it."

A certain degree of white-collar caution has always characterized Brokaw's organization. The great Huntley-Brinkley team, praised so much for its instant on-air chemistry, was an accident of the laboratory, the by-product of negotiations between two rival NBC forces each pushing its own man. Twenty years later Brokaw himself moved up to the anchor job as a kind of compromise between, on the one side, traditionalist factions loyal to the esteemed veteran John Chancellor and, on the other, more opportunistic, showbiz-minded executives willing to try something completely different to catch up with CBS—namely, the flash-and-dash communicator Tom Snyder. With the warring factions at NBC, Brokaw remembers, came "revolving-door leadership." Since he arrived in New York in the mid-seventies, first with "Today" and then with the "Nightly News," Brokaw has worked for six different NBC News presidents (as we saw, instability still reigns at NBC News). NBC wants to appear as the warm, "tasteful" network. Its biggest prime-time hit of the eighties was about a family, Bill Cosby's made-for-TV brood. During the second Reagan administration, Tom Brokaw was the host of the NBC Christmas broadcast that ended with Brokaw and Nancy Reagan, NBC's leading man and the nation's First Lady, singing Christmas carols on camera.

Like Rather, Tom Brokaw came out of the heartland. His terrain, however, was that of the contemporary split level, not the log cabin. Brokaw grew up in South Dakota, where his father was a construction foreman for the U.S. Army Corps of Engineers (the kind of job that would have made him Rags Rather's supervisor). Brokaw was very much the boy next door who marries his high school sweetheart. Her name was Meredith Auld, and she was the kind of girl who wins the Miss South Dakota title in the Miss America competition. In the late sixties and early seventies, when Brokaw was working for KNBC in Los Angeles, the Brokaws ran with a well-to-do Southern California crowd; he still serves on the board of the Norton Simon Museum of Art in Pasadena. He also ran on his own, apart from any pack. He became a jogger, he remembers, long before it became a craze, slogging through the Los Angeles streets in high tops, a lone runner in a town on wheels. Arriving in New York for NBC, neither Brokaw broke stride. He became a friend of Thornton Bradshaw, chairman of RCA, then the parent company of NBC. Meredith Brokaw started Penny Whistle, a chain of children's toy stores, where one birthday balloon sells for $1.50—without the air ("That's her business," he says amiably, "not mine").

Brokaw competed with Rather once before and lost. Both were covering the Nixon White House during the final days of the Watergate scandal, a time of some of Rather's best work. In the current round of competition, Brokaw for a time had the momentum. His program gained about 2 million viewers in the mid-1980s, while Rather was losing several hundred thousand. It is necessary to say "almost" and "about," because TV ratings, unlike the circulation figures for newspapers and magazines, are notoriously slippery. Ratings books come with qualifying asterisks sprinkled throughout like a measles rash. There are other services beside Nielsen—Arbitron, for example—as well as the networks' own research, and the numbers often differ. Then, too, ratings are affected by everything but the phases of the moon (and some have wondered about lunar influences as well). There is the "Wheel of Fortune" factor: some local stations displaying Vanna White in late-afternoon syndication pull large audiences away from the network news on other channels. There is also the role of lead-in shows; for example, the local ABC news programs in Chicago and Philadelphia, two of the top six television markets, attract a large number of viewers, helping build audiences for "World News Tonight." There is NBC's "Today" in the morning and the Cosby megahit in prime time; both may keep certain kinds of viewers tuned to NBC, in line with the TV law of inertia: a dial set at rest remains at rest unless acted upon by an outside intelligence. Finally, ratings can be a matter of how the ball bounces, literally. West Coast basketball play-off games and key baseball matchups have preempted network news shows in the last several years and helped change the ratings numbers. As Brokaw says, "There's no fixed formula for rating success. I've been down, and I've been up." Which one of these multiple factors decisively causes the variations? Check the correct answer and step up and claim a network-news presidency, paying in the low seven figures. The sensible view is that ratings success comes from a combination of elements—all of the above, but also the *substance* of the newscasts. For example, Robert Bazell on NBC has done the best reporting on AIDS, while Allen Pizzey on CBS has dominated South African coverage.

And then there is the anchor. The personality of the leading man is perhaps the only factor that evening-news producers can control. The White House and other officials determine when news is made; the affiliates and station owners are in charge of lead-ins and lead-outs; topography and neighboring buildings can affect the clarity of the picture. But the anchor allows for enterprise. As Brokaw says, "People watch people. They'll watch me as long as I deliver the kind of news they want and need." Brokaw's kind of news is centrist. "NBC Nightly News" did farm-crisis stories along with the others. But in search of its own angle, NBC went to the county seat of Cedar County, Nebraska, to see how the shoemaker and other small businesses serving the farmers were being affected. The people who look to NBC for news, according to Brokaw, "live in Walla Walla and El Paso, and they don't get the *New York Times* or the *Washington Post* or the *Wall Street Journal*." If Rather's heart has gone back to Texas's deep country and Jennings has moved toward the urban centers, Brokaw talked to the main streets of small cities and commuter towns, where in the 1980s the country's political and consumer power resided. Television news is obviously a mass activity engaging large demographic groups across a broad population. But just as clearly, each of the three anchors speaks to special constituencies. In the last years of the Reagan era, Brokaw had the growing audience. By the midterm mark in the first Bush administration, Jennings had taken over the lead.

Perhaps the audience grew weary of Brokaw, as it had of Rather. Perhaps it sensed something it did not like. Several years ago, Brokaw gave an interview to *Mother Jones*, the left-radical magazine published monthly in San Francisco. Brokaw had just been named the sole anchor of the "Nightly News," amid some sniping that he was just another pretty boy. "I wanted to demonstrate that I had been around politically," he recalls. Brokaw waded into the interview with some sharp comments about Reagan, whose values, he said, were "simplistic." Further, journalists were letting Reagan get away with "the crock that he was out of work in the '30s" and therefore knew what being poor was like. "He's always been a guy who had a paycheck coming in, an extremely rich man who has lived this isolated life . . . in this artificial world, with Nancy out in Pacific Palisades." The interview drew media attention all over the country. If Brokaw's audience cared, it did not show at the time; his ratings continued to go up. So did Reagan's. A lot of people saw nothing wrong with privilege. Reagan's vote-getting vision of the "shining city on a hill" was upscale, not so much a Norman Rockwell America as a vision of Beverly Hills, scaled to the suburbs.

Now, in the Bush years, realignments are taking place. Network news is still done in high-technology style and, most of the time, with journalistic substance. In the past few years, however, the same technology that makes it possible for the seven o'clock news to bring in satellite stories from all over the world also permits strong local stations and new cable networks to gather the same stories—and put them on the air 30 minutes or an hour before the network news comes on. More and more of the audience is deciding not to wait for Dan, or Peter, or Tom. Increasing numbers may turn to Ted Turner's Cable News Network, news set to the viewer's schedule rather than the networks'. Rather, Jennings, and Brokaw, and their bosses, have all begun to speculate on the next major change in television news. One new format under discussion involves bringing newsmakers on-camera and offering interviews or confrontational exchanges. Rather, Jennings, and Brokaw have all begun to do some of this within the structure of their present programs. But, as they and their viewers well know, the place where this emerging form gets its most prominent exercise is on ABC's "Nightline" with Ted Koppel and, in a more leisurely workup, on public broadcasting's "MacNeil/Lehrer News Hour." The present three-way split in the news audience among Rather, Jennings, and Brokaw serves them well, and keeps them in power, however uneasy lie their crowns. As local and cable alternatives presented themselves, the anchors' constituencies further weakened. The way was open for a new consensus personality to arise, not necessarily an authority figure like Cronkite or a demographic mirror like the current three but something much more, well, televisionlike. That is, a personality who thrives on live, unscripted, give-and-take controversy. As interviewers and creators of confrontation, Rather, Jennings, and Brokaw are simply not as good as Ted Koppel.

All three of the anchors, unlike one another in so many ways, agree on one thing: they see themselves as newsmen, reporters who can go out and get that story, and not as mere readers of the news. By the mid-1990s, they might be surprised, albeit pleasantly, if they are to be believed, to find themselves back on the streets again.

CNN: The News on Demand

6

When a chartered DC-8 carrying troopers of the U.S. 101st Airborne Division home for the holidays crashed at dawn in Gander, Newfoundland, on a December day in 1985, the news organizations of ABC, CBS, and NBC reported the story as it developed on their morning interview shows. Once regular daytime programming began, however, only occasional bulletins broke into the stream of game shows and soaps. But viewers tuned in to the Cable News Network heard the first reports during "Daybreak," the network's morning news show, and received new information continually all day. CNN was also the first U.S. network to show scenes from the crash site, using videotape supplied by the Canadian Broadcasting Corporation (CBC), at 11:23 A.M. (EST).

CNN, Ted Turner's vision of an all-news network broadcasting 24 hours a day, went on the air in 1980; in ten years the CNN staff has grown from 500 to over 2,000. At a time when the three major networks have been trimming their budgets and closing overseas bureaus, CNN has opened news bureaus in Nairobi, Frankfurt, Paris, New Delhi, and Beijing. Live and taped footage, made available through agreements negotiated with other national news organizations, such as CBC, as well as with over 185 local U.S. stations, enables CNN to select with some care the stories it puts on the air. "In the beginning, we had to scramble to fill

24 hours of air time," a CNN editor in the Washington bureau says. "Now we can be concerned with quality." CNN's scrambling days are historic memories today; one measure of its current status can be found in the fact that NBC tried to buy a share of the operation in 1988 (the plan fell apart when Turner and NBC could not agree on the question of who would have editorial control). But does CNN measure up to its competition in terms of quality? What distinguishes it from its older, bigger rivals? What do cable subscribers get when they tune to CNN, and what is the other third—the one in every three U.S. households still without cable—missing?

The most straightforward way to begin to answer such questions is by comparing the outputs of these news organizations. My associates at New York University helped me monitor CNN coverage over several weekly periods in the mid- and late 1980s. We contrasted the 24-hour cable service with the morning and evening news offerings of ABC, CBS, and NBC. To avoid comparing apples and oranges, we restricted our analyses to the "showcase" news programs of ABC, CBS, NBC, and CNN, leaving out the interview shows, such as "Nightline," "Larry King Live," and "Meet the Press," and the special-interest programs (for example, CNN's "Moneyline"). To be sure we were being fair in our judgments, we used two methods to keep score. First, we "randomly accessed" all four networks, the way a viewer might before leaving the house for work in the morning or after returning home in the evening. Second, we systematically analyzed the morning and evening newscasts: ABC's "Good Morning America" and "World News Tonight"; the "CBS Morning News" and the "CBS Evening News"; the NBC "Today" show and the "NBC Nightly News"; and CNN's premiere morning and evening news programs, "Daybreak" (6:00–6:30 and 7:00–9:00 A.M. [EST] and "Primenews" (8:00–9:00 P.M.)

CNN was at its best on the "Big Event"—especially if it was breaking news. As the Newfoundland story showed, a network in the business of covering news 24 hours a day does not have to debate whether to interrupt its program schedule for plane crashes or hurricane watches. At CNN, the schedule accommodates the information, not the other way around. ABC, CBS, and NBC covered the Newfoundland accident in detail during their nightly newscasts, but for anyone wanting to know what was going on from midmorning through early evening, CNN provided the news. It has been through such breaking news stories that CNN has shed its earlier soft image (in its early days it was disparaged as the "Chicken Noodle Network"). After Soviet fighter planes shot down Korean Air Lines Flight 007 in 1983, for example, CNN alertly broadcast the news briefing by the Soviet defense ministry in Moscow, an unprecedented first in 40 years of television news. Free of the ironlike programming vise on the older networks' evening news, which allows just 22 minutes for the world after commercials are subtracted, CNN has the expertise to handle live, developing stories routinely. Correspondent Mary Alice Williams recalls that when she was the anchor for CNN's "Newswatch," a 90-minute live summary of the day's events, starting at 5:00 P.M. (EST), she reported live on more than a dozen air crashes in a four-year period. (Her on-air work was so good that she attracted the attention of NBC and was hired away from CNN in 1989.)

Perhaps CNN's finest moments came at the outbreak of the war in the Persian Gulf in January 1991. The initial fighting was brought live into American homes by the satellite technology of CNN. The cable network's triumph in those first weeks changed American TV-news coverage, even if the other established networks did not immediately recognize the new landscape. CNN provided a continuous flow of raw but serviceable news—from the Pentagon, the White House, Riyadh, Amman, Tel Aviv, and Baghdad. Viewers had access to real-time information: the live briefings, the lengthy interviews and—yes—the censored dispatches and the outright propaganda, from all sides. In a way only beginning to be understood, the technology of instant international communications changed long-standing relationships among official newsmakers, news carriers, and news audiences.

With a large *scheduled* event, such as the first Geneva summit meeting of Ronald Reagan and Mikhail Gorbachev in 1985, CNN's advantages of time and accessibility may be negated. ABC, CBS, and NBC spent more money for their Geneva coverage—well over $1 million a week compared to CNN's $845,000, by one CNN executive's estimate. Also, in our Geneva monitoring week of 18–22 November, we found that the older networks' evening newscasts devoted a larger portion of their time to the summit than did CNN's. While ABC, CBS, and NBC spent up to 75 percent of the 22-minute newscast (after commercial time is subtracted) on the summit, CNN's "Primenews" gave just over 10 minutes, about 20 percent of its time, to Geneva. CNN did devote several hours out of its total schedule to Geneva events during the summit week, yet "Primenews" made little attempt to do either background or perspective pieces about any of the major issues then dividing the two superpowers: the Star Wars scheme, nuclear arms, Afghanistan, human rights, and Central America, among others. ABC, CBS, and NBC did do some light stories—taking time for the almond tea party with Nancy Reagan and Raisa Gorbachev, for example, and offering features on the media's coverage of the summit (the press looking at the press). But the older networks also did newsworthy background pieces. In particular, CBS broadcast a strong report on Afghanistan during the summit week. ABC featured the American commentator George Will and Gennady Gerasimov, then the editor-in-chief of the weekly newspaper *Moscow News,* head-to-head on "World News Tonight"; the same program also examined how the press of the Soviet Union and the Warsaw Pact nations were reporting the summit. Meanwhile, CNN's "Primenews" remained with its format of hard news interspersed with financial and medical/science reports, and non-Geneva features; for example, CNN's "Looking Up" segment, a two-to-three minute "happy news" report, on 10 November showed toddlers making fettuccine. On 18 November "Primenews" featured a story about the firing of the cheerleaders for the Chicago Bears football team.

"Primenews" occasionally provided longer stories than the networks, but longer did not necessarily mean more informative. CNN editors became enamored with the "human drama" of a Soviet seaman trying to defect. They did two stories on a subpoena delivered to a Soviet ship anchored in the Mississippi River; the papers demanded that the Soviets hand over the seaman, Miroslav Medved, to U.S. authorities for questioning. The Soviets refused to do so, and CNN reported on the Soviet's position and the U.S. reaction. The stories ran two minutes and one minute, 30 seconds, respectively. "NBC Nightly News" covered the same story but cut down on some footage—for example, Americans protesting the Soviets' actions—with no significant loss of information; its single story ran just one minute, 30 seconds. Mostly, "Primenews" used its "extra time"—compared to the networks' evening newscasts—for padding: weather, sports, and other soft features that viewers usually find on a good local newscast in Boston, Los Angeles, or Chicago.

CNN's "Daybreak" delivers mostly hard news and contrasts sharply with the magazine format and half-hour headline services of CBS's "Morning News," NBC's "Today," and ABC's "Good Morning America." During the summit, "Daybreak" broadcast both live press briefings and extensive taped coverage. The briefings made for excellent television, providing a real sense of the fabric of summit meetings and what the day in Geneva was like. CNN-watchers saw White House press briefings, complete with all the bickering between Reagan spokesman Larry Speakes and the White House press corps. Antagonists on a first-name basis, press secretary and press corps argued like an old married couple who know each other's crotchets by rote. CNN did not draw back from the live broadcasts that convey the normal tedium of newswork, and so CNN viewers were able to watch, in too-real time, what Washington correspondents and television technicians usually do all day: wait endlessly for the president or some other official to arrive, record the pro forma statements, and watch the newsmaker climb aboard Air Force One.

When a major event is scheduled in advance, the older networks can be found waiting alongside CNN. Mikhail Gorbachev's news conference on the last day of the summit began at 10:00 A.M. Geneva time. CNN carried it live, but so did ABC, CBS, and NBC, since it was 4:00 A.M. (EST) back at the networks' headquarters, with no high priority programming to interrupt. Had the Soviets scheduled their conference during the networks' prime entertainment time, or their affiliates' local—and equally profitable—news time, then CNN would have had the event to itself. Overall, CNN did a commendable job at Geneva. Its reporting was fair and accurate, without gimmicks or a lot of quasi news. While CNN did not provide extensive background, its stories were well edited, though without the polished look and slick graphics of its rivals. CNN's "Primenews" with its dual-anchor desks in Atlanta and Washington inevitably created the impression of a hybrid newscast, something between local and national news. The morning "Daybreak" news was much stronger and more news-oriented, without fettucine recipes or celebrity interviews.

Looking at CNN during other weeks in November and December, we detected some other areas where CNN is weaker than the networks. One was in news judgment. Most of the time the traditional evening newscasts have the same event as the lead news story, or at least as one of the first three stories. This can be taken as proof of an objective news sense—or as evidence of pack journalism. On 7 November, for example, ABC, CBS, and NBC began their shows with taped reports from Bogota, Colombia, where, the day before, political terrorists had taken over the Supreme Court building. The visuals showed a dramatic siege and a rising body count—objectively, a good television news story. CNN had offered live coverage of the seizure on "Newswatch" at 5:30 P.M. (EST). On CNN's "Primenews," however, that story did not appear until the middle of the program, after stories about the sailor Medved and a Romanian seaman who also attempted (successfully) to gain asylum in the United States.

Such news judgments give a further tilt to "Primenews," making it seem "local." Hurricanes, for example, get a lot of attention on CNN, as do farm stories. CNN's headquarters is in Atlanta, rather than within the New York–Washington news axis. CNN claims that this siting is one of its advantages: "It gets us out of the megalopolis point of view," said Christine Dolan, at the time a producer in CNN's Washington bureau. But the true extent of CNN's "outsider" status has been challenged. Daniel Schorr, the veteran newsman who worked for CNN in its early years, claims that he broke with Ted Turner in part because CNN's news operation covered business leaders who were later solicited by the network for advertising (a charge that Turner has denied). For the record, CNN's business interview segments seemed no softer than anyone else's when we looked at them. CNN's efforts to go beyond the usual Capital Beltway news judgments can be measured. When CNN broadcast a report on farm foreclosures, it gave this heart-tugger, a standard of mainstream journalism, a fresh appeal; instead of hearing about white, middle-class corn growers in Iowa, viewers learned of the plight of Oscar Lorik, a black peanut farmer from Georgia.

The generally flat, unremarkable level of the writing of CNN newscasts also contributed to our initial feeling of a network not-quite-ready for prime time. This is unsurprising given the low pay of CNN's Atlanta staff compared to salaries paid to ABC, NBC, and CBS staffers in New York and Washington. With the passage of time and the force of habit, we found less bothersome one of the more obvious distinctions between CNN and the networks: the Cable News Network lacks a single, strong personality. There is no Dan Rather or Peter Jennings or Tom Brokaw who personifies CNN, or gives it a distinct identity. CNN's regular news programs are anchored by a half dozen male-female teams, who come across as interchangeable. The absence of a star vehicle on CNN makes the news rather than the faces the focus of the camera—properly so for an all-news channel. Both because of its ample programming time and journalistic inclination, CNN can convey the news process, and not just the "product." CNN has in a way become the "network of record," sensibly stressing the importance of the news rather than the star appeal of the messenger.

CNN has been weak in the area of editorial commentary. John Chancellor on NBC and Bill Moyers, then with CBS, were particularly effective during the Geneva summit week. Without anyone to match their knowledgeability from Geneva, CNN fell back on the technique of commentary in the form of "crossfires," a CNN staple that encourages standard-issue liberals and conservatives to flame at each other. The matchup of the former U.S. congressman, and Jesuit priest, Robert Drinan and the fundamentalist minister Jerry Falwell made for "good TV," though it provided little insight, for example, on the New Right's view of summit meetings.

To sum up, a 24-hour news service is an idea whose time has come. Basically, viewers can get the news at their convenience from CNN. For those who can wait, ABC, CBS, and NBC's evening newscasts give the best concise packages of information. For straight, no-frills morning news, CNN's "Daybreak" is the choice. Interestingly, morning is the lowest-rated period of CNN's day, indicating that most people want their morning news and features over easy, in the style of the other networks, as in an order of breakfast eggs. CNN also offered the most substantial national news on Sunday nights, a not unimportant consideration. Unfortunately for CNN, its audience by the time of its tenth anniversary in 1990 still did not approach those watching news on the old-line networks. The fact that such large population areas as Washington, D.C., and Philadelphia have been slow to be wired for cable works against CNN. Nevertheless, by mid-1990 CNN was available in 54 million U.S. homes, and in 7 million more households abroad. CNN could also be seen in Beijing hotel rooms, as well as in Tokyo hotels and offices. Saddam Hussein's Iraqi Ministry of Information pirated the CNN signal from neighboring Jordan. Yassir Arafat and the Palestine Liberation Organization had a satellite dish outside PLO headquarters in Tunisia to steal the CNN signal as well. Castro in Cuba is known to be a CNN watcher. CNN is carried on one of the four television channels in Greece. It is on the pay channel in Nairobi. Officials in the Kremlin also have access to the CNN signal. At Gostelradio, the Soviet state radio and television authority, CNN broadcasts are regularly culled for videotape, to be used as visual materials on "Vremya," the main Soviet television news program.

In 1980, before CNN sent out its first signal, Ted Turner, with characteristic brass, called his creation "the world's most important network." Ten years later, he no longer sounds so megalomaniacal.

The Education of Diane and Sam

7

ABC News executives went down a long list of titles for their new weekly news hour, discarding names like "Perspective" and "Focus" before hitting upon "Prime Time Live." No one concerned thinks it is a very catchy name, but it really does not matter. The cohosts of "Prime Time Live," which had its premiere in August 1989, were Diane Sawyer and Sam Donaldson, and everyone realized that the program would survive or die as "The Diane and Sam Show." The celebrity of the hosts assured that conclusion. Sawyer was the Golden Girl of broadcasting, lured away from CBS after a protracted struggle waged by ABC News president Roone Arledge, who promised her greater stardom; Donaldson was the Bad Boy of the White House, who bayed at Ronald Reagan through eight years of otherwise genial news conferences and Rose Garden photo opportunities. For anyone who did not remember much about Sawyer's or Donaldson's on-camera work, the press accounts about their new contracts grabbed immediate attention. Sawyer was being paid $1.6 million a year, Donaldson a comparable sum.

But something more than the pulling power of two media stars was on the line when the lights went up on the sleek set of "Prime Time Live." The show appeared in the summer of the old-line networks' discontent, a time when their share of the total television audience had been dropping steadily with no signs of slowing. The Sawyer-Donaldson program and similar prime-time news efforts such as CBS's "48 Hours" represented the old-line networks' latest defensive strategy against their competitors. News shows in the prime evening hours have become their last redoubt. While it was not quite desperation time for the networks, programs like "Prime Time Live" signified "the recognition of the impossibility of finding first-rate entertainment series in appreciable numbers on a steady basis," as one ABC senior executive put it. The new business-minded ownership is ready to try anything, news included.

At ABC, the search for attractive entertainment programming has been especially frustrating. For every successful "Roseanne" or "thirtysomething," a dozen series fail each season. What's more, when a new comedy or dramatic show falters, replacement series have to be found by December or January (and perhaps again in the spring). Prime-time news programs are less expensive to produce; on average, they cost $300,000 each, compared with $800,000 and up for an entertainment show. They also do not require the creativity of a Chekhov every week. Mainly, they need news to play off: events can write the scripts. In the case of "Prime Time Live," the network's pressing need for an hour's worth of "product" to compete against NBC's strong "L.A. Law" and CBS's long-running "Knots Landing" came before the idea of the show itself and well before either Sawyer or Donaldson became available. The product, obviously, had to be shaped into some form and given an appealing face—or, this time, two faces. With its "20/20," ABC already had a successful weekly format, using standard magazine-style taped segments: Barbara Walters interview, investigative story, human-interest feature. ABC's "Nightline" was a solid achievement with, typically, one news story explored with bulldog tenacity by Ted Koppel, a genuine television talent. Diane Sawyer's previous assignment at CBS was as a correspondent for "60 Minutes," the model for an ensemble news show; CBS *invented* the form in 1967 and the program continued to roll on into the 1990s. For ABC to repeat itself or to copy another show would not make much journalistic sense; neither did such caution promise commercial success.

Arledge and two of his associates, Phyllis McGrady and Dorrance Smith, thought they had a way to differentiate their new program from other shows and appeal to the more playful mood of the audience. It is called "prime time," after all, because large numbers of viewers have tuned in seeking some kind of relaxation between the civic obligation of watching the evening news and the need to check sports results, tomorrow's weather, and late developments on the 11:00 P.M. local news. In prime time, the prime-time rules apply, and the talent is paid prime-time salaries. The rules also require high production values, good music, well-lit sets, and some quickly grasped concept like that of "L.A. Law" (lawyers and sex) or "Knots Landing" (sex and sex).

ABC had the stars. It also thought it had the simple concept: a live broadcast that would create excitement by going to the scene of the big events of the moment. "L.A. Law" and "Knots Landing" provided titillation, but they were taped dramas (and, for half the year, repeat shows). "Prime Time Live" would be real-time news. It would also be a homecoming for Arledge: he made his first major contributions to ABC as the producer in charge of its Olympics broadcasts. "Prime Time Live" was intended to cover the world, Arledge said, in much the same way ABC covered the Olympic Games: from multiple sites. For the roles played by the Olympics hosts Jim McKay and Keith Jackson—commenting on the action as it unfolds, adding their analyses and color—Arledge had Sawyer and Donaldson. And out in the field, at one or another global location, were the correspondents for "Prime Time Live": the able Chris Wallace, who as NBC's White House man competed against Donaldson, and Judd Rose, from "Nightline." They were going to do "Wide, Wide World of News." Their program would not be like any other news show on television. In particular, they were going to avoid looking like "60 Minutes." "Prime Time Live," Sawyer promised, would not be "three taped pieces 15-minutes long, with an Andy Rooney commentary at the end. We've told ourselves the canned broadcast is our enemy."

"Prime Time Live" did start with a distinctive look: live pickups from around the world, live unscripted interviews, spontaneous cross-talk between Sawyer and Donaldson, all taking place before a live studio audience that was invited to express its opinions. The program had to be lively, its creators thought, to appeal to the entertainment-minded television audience. So much for the plan. Within four months of its premiere, "Prime Time Live" had a new, yet strangely familiar, look. The global wizardry was more subdued; the Sawyer-Donaldson cross-talk consisted of little more than "Good evening, Sam," and "Good night, Diane," and the studio audience had all but disappeared from the screen. Most important of all, long videotaped pieces had grown to dominate the show. "Prime Time Live," in short, began to look like "the enemy."

How did "Prime Time Live," which was supposed to change the face of the news, come to be "Son of 60 Minutes"? One short answer is that there are just a few ways to do good journalism, and many ways to do bad journalism. From the start, the comments from the live audience added up to dead air time. The "simple idea" of being live turned out to be enormously draining on the staff. Producers were on the road constantly, Sawyer traveled to Cambodia, Wallace to Moscow; the pressure was, always, "where are we going next week?" The Sawyer-Donaldson exchanges at the end of the programs became painful to watch. "Prime Time Live" suffered by comparison with ABC's successes. When Donaldson and Sawyer did live interviews, someone remembered seeing Ted Koppel do it better. Their cross-talk was measured against the Sunday-morning exchanges of David Brinkley and George Will. Their celebrity interviews were flat in comparison to what Barbara

Walters achieved. The *New York Times* pondered whether there was "sufficient on-air chemistry" between Sawyer and Donaldson to carry the program.

On-air chemistry—the mix of personal qualities that appeals to audiences—has never been quantified. "Good chemistry is what turns out to work, retrospectively," says Richard Wald, senior vice-president at ABC News. "Prime Time Live" did well when it had some fresh news and information to impart. Among the most emblematic of the stories that appeared in the revised version was Judd Rose's report in November 1989 on David Duke, the former KKK grand dragon who had been elected to the Louisiana state legislature. The Duke piece had all the classic TV magazine elements: videotape of Duke in his Klan robes, interviews with Duke supporters and critics, analysis of how he had cleaned up parts of his act, "trading in his sheet for a suit," Rose reported. Nothing more had to be said. But Duke was brought into the studio anyway for a live interview, and Donaldson succeeded in making the unthinkable thinkable: his prosecutor's overkill created sympathy for the devil.

The two halves of the Duke segment illustrate what has been wrong with "Prime Time Live" and what can be done to make it right, journalistically at least. The taped report told the audience all it needed to know: Duke still represents just one suburban New Orleans district, not a national movement. The Donaldson interview was justified mainly by the live format rather than by news values. The taped report alone, obviously, would have made "Prime Time Live" "like" other television magazine shows. But is there that much wrong with that?

In hindsight, it is clear that "Prime Time Live" would inevitably evolve in the direction of traditional narrative. Don Hewitt, who created "60 Minutes" and helped it become a perennial top-10 program on television, claims that he "knew from the first week" where ABC would have to go with "Prime Time Live."

Hewitt has a four-word explanation for the success of "60 Minutes": "The secret is, 'tell a good story.' Good writers have understood that since the Bible." Hewitt is not an uninvolved critic (Sawyer worked for "60 Minutes" before she left for "Prime Time Live"). Circumspectly, he expresses merely his "astonishment that people as smart as Diane and her colleagues didn't see what is self-evident about news programs."

The people responsible for "Prime Time Live" acknowledge that they may have been blinded by the dazzling technology at their fingertips. Now, says an executive associated with the show, "Good narrative pieces are very much on our minds." Producers and reporters alike conceded that there was too much emphasis on process—putting the picture on the air, racing around to give "this just in . . ." news—and not enough attention to substance. In the "old days" of the program, if major fighting had erupted in, say, San Salvador, the reaction would have been to order a camera crew to the scene. In late 1989, when a big rebel offensive began, the producers passed on the story.

"Prime Time Live" had come into being to fill the programmers' needs for a different "product" to put opposite the competition's popular programs. But the programmers failed to define the exact nature of that competition. On the night of 9 November 1989 the Berlin Wall came down, on camera. By any measure, "Prime Time Live" responded superbly, bringing events as they happened to viewers. Praise for the program rang through ABC corporate headquarters, yet the audience ratings were the worst in the program's short history. ABC had to look no farther than to its own news programs for an explanation. The early evening news shows on ABC (and on CBS and NBC) were almost completely given over to live coverage from Berlin. Moreover, these regular news shows had begun extensive coverage days before when East German officials signaled the collapse of their regime and its repressive policies. By 10:00 P.M. Thursday night, 9 November, a good part of the audience felt sufficiently informed and exalted. Some viewers apparently had experienced enough of the delirium; perhaps there were too many Tin Men in the audience, people like the character in *The Wizard of Oz* who had no heart. Whatever the reason, many viewers were Berlined-out, and they escaped over the wall to "L.A. Law" and other prime-time entertainment.

The creators of "Prime Time Live" can do relatively little about unresponsive hearts or souls. But they can cultivate their own work, and make it as humane as possible. Having discovered that a live format can be a problem, and not a program, they have returned to the basics of good reporting: writing and editing. It is a fallback position at once familiar and time tested, and not a bad place to be on any night of the week.

Case Studies

AIDS, Sex, and "Good Taste" 1: Practicing Unsafe Journalism

8

On the evening of 11 November 1985 NBC broadcast "An Early Frost," a made-for-television motion picture about a young AIDS victim. Following the program and late local newscasts, Tom Brokaw anchored an NBC News special report on AIDS. Late in that report, Brokaw offered a warning to his viewers. Four years after the first fatal infections had shown up in homosexual men and two full years after the *Annals of Internal Medicine*, among other medical journals, had pointed to the specific kind of sexual activity by which many of the early cases of Acquired Immunodeficiency Syndrome were transmitted, NBC News finally used the term "anal intercourse."

The audience survived this shock. In fact, the special report attracted twice the audience that usually watches "The Tonight Show," with Johnny Carson, in the same time period. It is not so certain that journalism has survived the shock of covering the AIDS crisis. While other major players in the story—the federal government, local officials, gay activists, medical authorities—contributed to some of the misunderstanding and confusion, journalism added its own contradictory practices and ambivalent attitudes. By speaking far too long in euphemisms and being squeamish about news coverage in the initial stages of the epidemic, journalists added another layer of confusion to an already complex medical narrative. Perhaps no one should be surprised. The AIDS story raises a number of serious questions for journalists, very few of them resolved by glib answers.

The AIDS story line has moved erratically, sometimes characterized by hope, more often shaped by fear and hysteria. At times the high level of excitement in some of the coverage has made it hard to determine where medical urgency ends and commercial considerations begin. "Now No One Is Safe from AIDS," *Life* magazine proclaimed on its July 1985 cover. At times the story has been overreported, as in the rivers of ink expended on the actor Rock Hudson and AIDS in Hollywood (including such headlines in the *New York Post* as "AIDS Hits More H'wood Stars" and "Actors Ban Kiss of AIDS"). At other times, it has been misreported, as in the big blood contamination scare of 1983, when the existence of 27 AIDS cases that could be traced to a system that provided 10 million blood transfusions that year created a crisis for the nation's blood banks. The alleged "Haitian connection" was equally egregious, erroneously targeting an entire group of immigrants on the basis of some flawed medical interviews. (In the early stages of the epidemic, Haitian immigrants to the United States had been named, along with homosexuals and drug users, as a major AIDS risk group. Later, U.S. health officials discovered that homosexuality and drug use are so strongly condemned by Haitian culture that Haitian AIDS victims would be unlikely to admit either. Officials belatedly began to reclassify Haitian victims into either the homosexual or drug-user categories.)

In covering the AIDS story, journalists have had to depend on official sources for much of their information. News stories could be only as informative as the officials' own knowledge—which for a long time was tragically inadequate. But there is one part of the AIDS story for which journalists alone are responsible: the language used to describe how the AIDS tragedy occurred. Immunosuppresive mechanisms and virology are not normal journalistic specialities. But words, their meanings and their use to express clear, unambiguous information, are the journalists' responsibility. How clearly were the plain facts about AIDS communicated? When my associates and I looked at the television, radio, and print coverage of AIDS in the early period of the epidemic, we observed a pervasive reticence, an evident embarrassment, in describing the sexual modes of transmission. We analyzed three separate periods of coverage when AIDS began to appear in news stories: March to August 1983, when AIDS-related deaths were reaching four a day nationwide and receiving wide media attention; July to September 1985, when Rock Hudson's condition became known and when the opening of the school year prompted AIDS-in-the-classroom stories; and October to December 1985, when the issue of "public sex" was being pressed by New York governor Mario Cuomo and New York City mayor Ed Koch.

In the first period of coverage we noted a strong tension between two journalistic sensibilities: interest in a good story and fear of offending viewers and readers. The "mystery epidemic" appealed to the news instincts of reporters; "Terrifying . . . mysterious . . . out of thin air," were among the words used by Tom Brokaw on "NBC Nightly News" in April 1983. But the homosexual "angle" made these same newspeople nervous, and aggressive newshounds became prim gentlemen and ladies. It was not until May 1983 that the "CBS Evening News" reported that sexual activity was one of the major ways by which AIDS was spread. Throughout this period, a Victorian sensibility pervaded the putative family medium of television. Except for hearing fleeting references to "personal contact" or "sexual intimacy" or the "bathhouse culture of cities like New York or San Francisco," a viewer could listen in vain for any hint of the details about the means of transmission. Print coverage in this period was substantially the same as television's. In 1983 the *New York Times* offered little specific explanation about how AIDS was sexually transmitted. In part, this was due to the scarcity of confirmed medical knowledge. *Times* stories during this period concentrated on reporting recent scientific research on the biological mechanism involved. The paragraphs describing AIDS victims were general: "The Public Health Service said 'high risk' donors included patients diagnosed with AIDS, sexual partners of AIDS patients, persons with AIDS symptoms, sexually active homosexual or bisexual men with multiple partners, Haitian entrants to the United States, current or past abusers of intravenous drugs and sexual partners of individuals at high risk for AIDS" ("Fear of AIDS Has Red Cross Discouraging Certain Donors," 7 March 1983). In another *Times* article ("Rare Virus May Have Link with Immunological Illness," 1 May 1983), readers encountered this description: "AIDS has been reported primarily among men with frequent and varied homosexual contacts." The *Los Angeles Times*'s coverage in this period also chose the safety of ambiguity. "The disease has struck particularly hard in the male homosexual population, where it is probably spread by sexual contact," the *Los Angeles Times* reported on 4 March 1983. A short time later, however, on 29 April 1983, *Los Angeles Times* medical writer Harry Nelson discarded euphemisms and became one of the first reporters to tell the simple facts: the risk of AIDS, Nelson wrote, "is associated with passive (receptive) anal intercourse, in contrast with active (insertive) anal intercourse or no anal intercourse." Later in the same story Nelson wrote of "the presence of the agent in the semen of the active partner which in turn is transmitted to the passive partner's bloodstream through breaks in the rectal membranes." Because Nelson was able to write this account in a general-interest daily newspaper, the logical question arises about the absence of similar accounts. One of the few we saw appeared in the *New York Times Magazine* on 6 February 1983, when a freelance writer, Robin Marantz Henig, described the possibility of contagion by "oral-anal or anogenital contact."

On radio, a somewhat different story emerged in this period. Although our monitoring could hardly be comprehensive—there are over 9,000 radio outlets in the United States, and few scripts are saved—we did find examples of more explicit talk about AIDS, in keeping with radio's usually less reserved style. For example, on 7 July 1983, NBC Radio presented a special report, "AIDS: Facts and Fears," in which correspondent Peter Laufer stated: "Because scientists don't know what causes the disease, or the exact way it spreads, there is understandable fear of the unknown." Laufer then let his interviewees do the talking. "The best one can suggest to avoid the disease is to avoid intimate sexual and blood-sharing contact with high-risk groups," said Dr. Anthony Fauci of the U.S. National Institutes of Health. Jim Graham, administrator of the Whitman-Walker Clinic in Washington, D.C., added, "I think you're going to witness, if the situation continues, increases in voyeurism, in masturbation, in body massage, and various other things which, you know, are nontraditional in terms of sexual activities for gays."

In our second period of monitoring, the *New York Times* took a step toward clarity by including medical explanations of how blood transfusion recipients and drug addicts contract AIDS. But those stories continued to omit specifics of how male homosexuals transmit AIDS through sexual intercourse. Stories printed during late July and early August 1985, for example, reported on a blood test that would detect the presence of AIDS virus antibodies in blood. Although only 2 percent of all recorded victims contracted AIDS through blood transfusions, contrasted to 60 percent who contracted it through sexual intercourse, considerable attention was given to the transfusion cause for infection. No detailed medical information about how AIDS was transmitted by other risk groups was reported. "Sexual contact" became the phrase for explaining how homosexual males contract AIDS: "The virus believed to cause the disorder is said to be transmitted either through sexual contact or through the blood," the *Times* reported on 20 August 1985. Other major newspapers used similarly vague language. A news account in the *Boston Globe* on 4 October 1985 explained AIDS as "acquired immune deficiency syndrome, which can be transmitted through bodily fluids, usually through sexual contact"; no specifics about "bodily fluids" were given. A *Washington Post* story on 27 July 1985 contained this paragraph: "[AIDS] is thought to be spread primarily through sexual contact, but may also be spread through contact with needles, blood, or other body fluids. It is not, however, thought to be spread through casual contact."

Beginning in mid-August and early September 1985, news organizations, as if collectively, seemed to take a deep breath and decide to mention the previously unmentionable. On 11 August 1985 a United Press International story from Washington reported that the United States Conference of Mayors had awarded $145,000 to eight cities for educational projects to inform the public about AIDS. The projects, UPI reported, will "urge sexual practices that avoid the exchange of bodily fluids, such as premature withdrawal or the use of condoms." The *New York Times* ran the UPI story. It was one of the few times we saw or heard the word "condom" during this period—though for several months gay bathhouses in New York and San Francisco had been routinely handing out, along with locker keys and "safe sex" literature, packets with condoms marked: "The contents of this envelope could save your life." In September, television decided to face some of the facts of life. Robert Bazell of NBC was consistently forthright and reliable, as well as ahead of his rivals, on the AIDS story; more than any other reporter he helped put to rest the so-called Haitian Connection to AIDS. Appearing on NBC's "Today" show on 9 September, he confronted the subject of AIDS by reporting: "I think that we have been squeamish . . . when we talk about AIDS. We talk about things like intimate contact and casual contact. You can get it from intimate contact, you can't get it from casual contact. And nobody really knows what that means." Turning to "Today" coanchor Bryant Gumbel, he asked, "Are you and I having intimate contact now or casual contact?" Bazell added, "The truth is, you get this disease mainly through sexual intercourse and primarily through anal intercourse as practiced by male homosexuals." Bazell also sharpened the language of AIDS reporting on the evening news—up to a point. On the "NBC Nightly News" on 16 September Bazell said, "How is AIDS spread? For a person to be infected, the virus must enter his bloodstream. Sexual intercourse, where semen enters the bloodstream, is the most common mode of transmission. Researchers know that the disease can be transmitted by homosexual men during intercourse." Somehow, the adjective "anal" was lost between Bazell's morning and evening broadcasts.

Although the press, during this period, was becoming more frank in its coverage of AIDS, many news organizations continued to report the story in conflicting ways. On 7 November 1985, New York City padlocked the Mine Shaft, a gay sex club in Greenwich Village, based on a new regulation of the state's Public Health Council; the regulation prohibited fellatio and anal intercourse—defined as "high-risk" activities, that is, AIDS-related—in public places. Authorities said they acted based on a report by city inspectors of what they had observed during their surveillance of the Mine Shaft during the first weekend of November. The *New York Daily News* ran an account of the inspectors' report in its early national edition of 8 November 1985. After what James Willse, at the time the paper's managing editor, called "heated debate," the next edition carried a shorter story, omitting some of the more explicit language. The newspaper *Newsday* in New York, with its city and suburb editions, became a textbook study of community standards. To its circulation audience of over 500,000 in affluent, suburban Long Island, *Newsday* offered a cleaned-up version of the inspectors' Mine Shaft report on page 17. New York *Newsday*, however, aimed at the grittier middle-class areas of

Queens, Brooklyn, and the Bronx, as well as "sophisticated" Manhattan, carried a longer version with a page-1 headline, "What the City Shut Down." *Newsday*'s urban readers could learn about incidents of "proscribed sexual encounters" that inspectors reported witnessing: "On November 3, 1985, anal intercourse was observed being engaged in by six patrons of the Mine Shaft in plain view of other patrons.... On November 3, 1985, fellatio was observed being engaged in by 22 patrons of the Mine Shaft in plain view of other patrons."

The reporting of the Public Health Council resolution, together with the Mine Shaft closing, marked a turning point for most "family" media. Till then local television news in New York had been opaque in its language. On 10, 11, and 12 July 1985 WNBC, the NBC-owned station in New York City, ran a three-part series on AIDS. The closest the report came to being explicit came when Dr. Philip Kayal, a sociologist, was quoted speaking at a community meeting in Brooklyn: "You simply have to learn how to refrain from the exchange of body fluids," he said in response to a comment about promiscuous sexual behavior. On 25 October, the day of the health council vote, WNBC anchor Pat Harper began the 6:00 P.M. broadcast by saying, "Good Evening, New York State has cleared the way to shut down gay bathhouses and other places that offer public sex while spreading AIDS." Then reporter Rolonda Watts said that the legislation affected "any establishment that may contribute to the spread of AIDS through oral or anal sex." Reporter Carol Jenkins, in the next story, spoke of "government restrictions on oral or anal sex." With those words—the result, we were told later, of much impassioned discussion among the staff of WNBC—the "tough" terms were out in the open, and a new level of language was becoming more familiar in all the media.

Our group looked through an assortment of AIDS-related newspaper clips, magazine stories, radio and television scripts dating to 1982 to find any examples of language that was both clear and inoffensive to broad numbers of readers/viewers. Recognizing that degrees of acceptance differ from place to place, we decided that an article by John Langone in the December 1985 issue of *Discover* magazine constituted forthright yet tasteful communication. Langone wrote, "Anal sex is an essential element in the AIDS story, and recognition of that fact has affirmed what researchers suspected when the deadly malady surfaced more than four years ago: AIDS is a blood-borne disease that in most cases strikes, and will continue to strike, homosexual and bisexual males who have been the receptive partners in anal sex, a practice that tears the delicate lining of the rectum and allows the AIDS virus easy entry into the body's circulatory system." Equally clear information appeared in a question-and-answer box (accompanying an AIDS cover story) by Jean Seligmann and Mariana Gosnell in *Newsweek* on 23 September 1985: "*Q*: What are the risks for women? *A*: . . . the biggest risk for women (as for men) seems to be anal sex, which often involves tearing of the rectal lining and allows the virus easy entry into the bloodstream. Many researchers, in fact, believe that a tear in the skin is essential for the virus to be transmitted. They suggest that vaginal sex may be safer because the vagina's lining is thicker and more friction resistant than that of the anal canal." This was not shock for shock's sake. Langone, Seligmann, and Gosnell were veteran medical writers who were not interested in titillating their audience. Because they wrote for "upscale" special-interest magazines with presumably better-educated readers, they were perhaps less inhibited in their choice of words.

Supervising editors and news directors were the decision makers during the various stages of the AIDS story. These gatekeepers frequently invoke the image of a general-interest, broadly based audience as a factor limiting their judgments. Recalling the Mine Shaft transcript debate in the *Daily News* city room, editor Willse says: "Some editors felt it was our responsibility to carry details. It was impossible to shock our readers, they said. Others felt there was no need to be that precise. Some readership, however, is older and doesn't know or doesn't want to know what goes on in a gay bar." The paper, he says, carried medical stories and health science stories that used the words *rectum* and *semen*. Willse adds: "We don't feel it necessary, every time you write about AIDS, to say anal and oral sex." Jerry Nachman, WNBC's news director at the time, also worried about his audience, and his own discomfort. "I held my breath and winced," Nachman says of his station's coverage. "Part of the difficulties with this kind of epidemiological problem is euphemism," Nachman acknowledges. Although the words were clinical in context, he still found them "jarring and disorienting." If television news covers AIDS explicitly, then "someone in the audience calls me and says, 'My 8-year-old asked, Daddy, what's oral sex?' " As news director, Nachman found himself caught between the importuning of his worldly reporters and his concern for the tastes of his general audience, whose members included the very young and the old. "We had to balance educational and public health service benefits with the question of suitability for a dinner-hour news show. Remember, we're not really a classroom. My primary role is not educational." Other editors argued that readers should be given more credit for knowing what words like "sexual contact" mean without stories piling on graphic detail. At the *Washington Post*, medical writer Cristine Russell defended the paper's use of the word *intimate* on the grounds that "Intimate is general. It doesn't just mean sex. It also refers to mother and child transmission, sharing of needles, and blood transfusions." According to Russell, "intimate is a word that is suggestive to readers as the opposite of casual." For that matter, "Body fluids is not a mysterious word."

Journalists should not have to take all the responsibility for the timid language used in AIDS coverage. The habits and speech patterns of medical researchers, who speak in double negatives, statistical probabilities, and other hedge talk, contributed to vagueness. As Russell says, "A lot of articles reflect what we hear from experts and the language they choose to use." Richard Flaste, then the director of science news for the *New York Times*, also cites the initial lack of comprehensive medical knowledge about AIDS, as well as researchers' early disagreements about precise modes of transmission. "For a while, we did know it was associated with gay men and with their sexual activity. The issue of anal and oral sex and the relative danger of one versus the other arose only in the most speculative way. It was a matter of deduction. People think anal tears may contribute." The *Times* sees itself as keeping the AIDS story overall in balance. "While there is fear," Flaste says, "it may be overstated by scientists."

The question of risk, specifically the chances for an AIDS breakout into the heterosexual population, is addressed in the next chapter. Speaking only of the subject discussed here, the language of AIDS, media behavior is perhaps understandable. Several forces pushed AIDS coverage into a proper Victorian stance. The facts of the transmission of AIDS could not be treated in daily papers, general-interest publications, or on radio and television broadcasts without colliding with deeply rooted American social attitudes. There is a reticence, "a natural squeamishness about most things sexual," as Robert Bazell says. Despite significant changes in America in the last several decades, sex is still not a subject for wide public discussion. The wider society is still reluctant to look unblinkingly at homosexuality. Gay men and women have come out of the closet, but many people still want to keep the room lights dim. Two of Mayor Koch's presumably street-hardened inspectors declined, in the line of duty, to look in on the back rooms of the Mine Shaft. The Brokaws and Bazells must face an audience of 15 million Americans of varying age, education, and moral views. As Bazell says, "When you have a viewership that is the entire country, it becomes very difficult to know how to handle that." In fairness, too, it is important to point out that the announcements from the U.S. Centers for Disease Control and from other health groups have often been vague. Terms like "casual contact" and "intimate contact" were initially used by them as well. It was not as if the journalists were hearing graphic, descriptive material about sex from the scientists and then passed on a heavily censored version of the truth to their audience.

We may never know just how much of journalism's reticence, its opacities, euphemisms, and discreet tuggings of the window shades down on "too graphic" and/or "vulgar" materials contributed to public misunderstanding about AIDS. On several occasions prominent television journalists have appeared on camera with AIDS victims, to make a point of showing that the virus cannot be transmitted casually. Commendable as this kind of demonstration is, one explicit picture has not been worth a thousand too-cautious words.

AIDS, Sex, and "Good Taste" 2: Celebrity Journalism

9

"AIDS isn't a disease anymore," the playwright Harvey Fierstein has been quoted as saying, "it's a media event." He was being theatrical, of course. Fierstein knows as well as anyone that acquired immunodeficiency syndrome has reached epidemic proportions and will have killed 179,000 Americans by 1992, according to the United States surgeon general.

Still, Fierstein's comment excites the shock of recognition. Since AIDS the epidemic has become major news, AIDS the story has made troubling news. We have had celebrity coverage (Rock Hudson and Liberace), mystery (the cases of Roy Cohn and Perry Ellis), and ideology (the handling of the death of New Right activist Terry Dolan). More than any recent news story, the AIDS epidemic has raised questions about journalistic standards, confidentiality, and privacy. Both *People* magazine and the *National Enquirer* had issues on the newsstands and supermarket racks with stories about Liberace's "secret battle with AIDS" before the Riverside County, California, coroner had in fact concluded that the entertainer suffered from AIDS. AIDS was mentioned in fashion designer Perry Ellis's obituaries in the *Washington Post, USA Today, Newsday,* and *Newsweek,* but it was not mentioned in the *New York Times, Los Angeles Times,* or *Time.* Terry Dolan's death received extensive page-1 coverage in the conservative *Washington Times,* where his death was carefully attributed to congestive heart failure, a day before the liberal *Washington Post* could report the fact of Dolan's death.

In many respects, coverage of the last days of a Rock Hudson or a Liberace is no different from other celebrity-centered journalism. "Celebrity Drugs" and "Celebrity Divorce" also command airtime. Celebrity AIDS, though, offers an extra sensation: to the "drama" of death by incurable affliction—even the rich and famous aren't immune!—is added the shiver of sexual ambiguity. As long as AIDS kills prominent public figures, there will be media exploitation of celebrity deaths. The more disturbing media issue revolves, perversely, around the underreporting of AIDS. A generation ago, the word *cancer* almost never appeared in obituaries or news accounts of deaths. Because of ignorance and fear, an implicit social stigma was attached to the disease. Today, in many minds, AIDS registers an explicit, stronger aversion. It started out, after all, as "the gay plague." As a result, journalists are rethinking such previously routine tasks as writing about deaths, while readers and viewers must learn how to decode many news stories. Four cases from the late 1980s are worth examining.

1. *What the Doctor Said*   John Terrence "Terry" Dolan had been identified with the "family values" agenda of political conservatives and with the Reagan administration; his brother was the chief White House speechwriter. And so Dolan's death at 36 in late December 1986 became a major event. Dolan had denied that he was a homosexual, despite contrary reports. When he died after a long illness, a kind of news management—familiar in Washington—took place. The front-page tributes in the *Washington Times* were accompanied by a telephone campaign by Dolan's friends and colleagues that targeted the *Washington Post*. As a *Post* editor recalls it, "Everyone who knew anyone's number here called." The message callers wanted to get across was that Dolan's doctor had listed the cause of his death as congestive heart failure: if the *Post* reported that Dolan had suffered from AIDS, it would be mistaken and would be doing a disservice to Dolan's memory.

The *Post*, however, did its own phoning around and then ran a 22-inch story the next day, stating flatly and with no attribution that Dolan had suffered from AIDS. According to *Post* people, several factors influenced the decision. First of all, an "undisputed source" had said that Dolan suffered from AIDS. Further, Dolan's doctor acknowledged that he had never tested his patient for the AIDS virus and that he was not the only doctor treating Dolan. Also, as every medical reporter at the *Post* knew, no one "dies of AIDS." AIDS is a condition, not a disease, that allows other diseases to kill. The *Post* remains confident about its source. The Washington bureau of the *New York Times* had less success with the Dolan story. Pressed by New York editors to match or shoot down the *Post* account, the bureau came up empty-handed. The bureau had heard the rumors, a lot of people in Washington had. But, says Allan M. Siegal, a *Times* assistant managing editor, "We don't print scuttlebutt." Without an authoritative confirmation of the kind the Post had, or believed it had, "the *Times* to this day has not said Dolan had AIDS," according to Siegal.

2. *The "Authoritative" Source* Liberace and his friends and family also sought to control the news. As *People* wrote in its story, "Liberace's homosexuality had been one of the worst-kept secrets in show business, but he had guarded it until the end." Liberace had been the target of a so-called palimony lawsuit brought by Scott Thorson, his "personal chauffeur." There was a presumption in the media about Liberace's sexual preferences. Two weeks before Liberace's death, Hank Greenspun, the publisher of the *Las Vegas Sun*, ran a story declaring that Liberace, "longtime show-stopper on the Las Vegas Strip," was "terminally ill with AIDS." The *Sun* cited "informed sources." Greenspun, himself a major figure in Las Vegas, had known Liberace for decades; he also said he had access to medical records, documents supposed to be confidential, in Las Vegas and elsewhere.

When the performer's end came, Liberace's doctors gave the cause of death as cardiac arrest due to heart failure. It was true as far as it went: ultimately, we all die when our hearts stop. The doctors also acknowledged, after the coroner's report, that the AIDS virus was present in Liberace's blood. But a lot about AIDS is "far from defined," the doctors said, adding that they chose to stay with the narrowest interpretation of the facts to protect the privacy of Liberace and his family. Many papers, the *New York Times* among them, carried both the doctors' statement and the *Sun*'s report.

3. Private Rights, Public Rights   Unlike most papers, the *New York Times* does not run many obituaries (as opposed to death announcements, which are prepared and paid for by the deceased's survivors or the funeral home, and set in a different typeface). *Times* obituaries invariably involve well-known or clearly prominent people; three to five a day typically appear. When the deceased is, in Siegal's words, "a reasonably private figure," the *Times* will ask the survivors for the cause of death but will not aggressively pursue it. "We don't beat up on people," Siegal says. Because of questions of news judgment raised by the *Times*'s coverage of certain deaths in recent years, notably those of the lawyer Roy Cohn and the designer Perry Ellis, Siegal wrote down some guidelines for the staff. "If we know or can reliably learn a specific cause of death, we print it," his memo of 10 December 1986 stated. "If we lack the information, we try to learn it through all normal reporting methods. . . . If we suspect we are being given only a partial truth, we print it, with pointed and specific attribution to the source."

At the *Washington Post*, obituary policies are different, and *Post* stories reflect this difference. The *Post* regards itself as a hometown paper. When a Washington resident dies and the survivors telephone in the news, the paper tries to run an obituary, according to Richard Pearson, one of four reporters in the paper's obit "bureau." *Post* stories have a required format: age, cause of death, and survivors. Pearson and his colleagues insist on printing the cause of death for private and public figures alike. If callers, such as the deceased's family, or friends, or coworkers, resist these rules, they are asked to reconsider; if they still hold back information, they are told that there will be no obituary. With prominent figures, the obit writers pursue stories as any reporter would. Pearson wrote the story on Roy Cohn's death. Cohn had denied having AIDS—to Mike Wallace on the CBS program "60 Minutes," no less. But in Cohn's last days, he was being treated at the U.S. National Institutes of Health with an experimental drug whose sole use, says Pearson, "was to fight AIDS, and we said that in our story."

4. Drawing the Line Some AIDS sufferers and their families see beyond the AIDS stigma. The day that the *Times* carried an Associated Press story describing the California coroner's concern about a Liberace cover-up, it also carried a short obituary on the death of a 45-year-old producer who had died of AIDS, "according to his family." Not everyone is so enlightened. Complex interests, institutional as well as familial, may come into play in AIDS coverage. In the magazine *Vanity Fair*, a two-page photographic spread commemorated AIDS victims in fashion and the arts. Editor-in-chief Tina Brown wrote that she knew of several creative people who were infected with AIDS. Brown explained that she would not identify them, as the magazine did the deceased, for to do so might damage their ability to continue to earn a living and pay their medical bills. This need for anonymity was "a sad commentary on the world," she concluded.

Distinctions between the living and the sick do not always work. Perry Ellis the designer may have died in May 1986, but Perry Ellis designs remain a $260-million-a-year enterprise. Again, there had been gossip about Ellis's sexuality. When he died at 46 (of viral encephalitis, according to the hospital), the *Los Angeles Times* obituary was written by its fashion editor, Bettijane Levine. According to Levine, she omitted any mention of AIDS, because after "at least 45 phone calls," she could not "get anyone to confirm authoritatively" that Ellis had AIDS. Friends protected Ellis's memory, and, not so incidentally, a prestigious fashion label. Patricia Morrisroe of *New York* magazine spent two months researching the Ellis story, interviewed 52 people, and concluded that "many people believe Ellis had AIDS, and given the evidence, it seems likely."

The obituary notice in our time has become a new battleground. Homosexual groups ask for a full reporting of AIDS deaths, if for no other reason than to give heterosexuals a sense of the magnitude of the epidemic, and spur more support for AIDS research and treatment. The cases of stonewalling and denial recounted here have led some writers to argue that there may be a distinction between being "gay" and being "homosexual": gays identify socially and politically, and therefore publicly, with their sexual orientation; homosexuals choose to suppress that identity, to control a carefully cultivated public image, in life and, if possible, in death.

The media have to protect their own image. The most open way is by avoiding sexual politics of any kind, thus steering clear of being perceived as squeamish or part of a cover-up, gay or straight, left or right. Energetic reporting, together with full disclosure of the causes of death when public figures die, creates fewer ethical problems than the tactics of avoiding mention of AIDS. Allan Siegal says, "It is journalism to print what you can find out." In short: Put it in the paper and put it on the air.

High on Crack

10

Vietnam was the first living-room war, its scenes of death carried into American homes by the reach of television. In the same way, cocaine—particularly in its cheaper, smokable form know as crack—became our first living-room drug.

Television brought crack home beginning in the summer of 1986. The coverage on the three commercial networks powerfully shaped perceptions of both the danger of crack use and its prevalence in American cities and towns. But how accurate were the impressions that the viewers received? A study of the initial coverage of the "crack epidemic," compared to the then-available facts, suggests that the alarms and excursions about a new nationwide plague of cocaine addiction were exaggerated.

The battle against drugs as a "living-room war" was a simile that television journalists themselves were quick to pick up. As Dan Rather announced, introducing the "CBS Evening News" on 2 September 1986: "Tonight, CBS News takes you to the streets, to the war zone for an unusual two hours of hands-on horror. Our focus is on crack; a kind of cocaine, a powerful mind bender and increasingly popular and deadly." Then followed a three-minute, 40-second preview of the two-hour prime-time special to be broadcast later that night. As with Vietnam, so too with crack. Viewers of the special report saw quick, jarring cuts of the combat action, including hidden-camera shots of illicit buys on street corners, often taking place at night with neon signs casting nightmarish colors and with sirens wailing in the distance. There were interviews with grim officials who projected more cases. Crack addicts, we learned, will "do anything" to get another fix. We were in a war zone recast in the Day-Glo colors of a music video. Yet, during the news coverage of the "crack summer of 1986," the mesmerizing images appearing on the TV screen in many respects diverged from the crack reality. The CBS preview, for example, alerted viewers with a line declaring that Crack Street could be "your street." This statement was way off the mark: the evidence remains that crack has been a serious problem only in certain large metropolitan areas, including the media centers of New York and Los Angeles. While use of crack could well have been on the increase in 1986, it may be that the use was mostly among those *already* using cocaine and other drugs. The "crack summer of 1986," then, can best be explained by looking at the news system—and its own addictive habits.

Media attention to crack fit a familiar journalistic pattern: first, a base-line period of "normal" mention of drug stories from March through May 1986; second, the sound-and-fury stage of June, July, and August, when crack and cocaine stories received more than five hours of coverage on the networks' evening news shows; third, a period of reaction in the following three months, with far fewer "combat zone" stories and a realization that the coverage might have gone too far. In this reflective phase, the media coverage of crack became a story in itself. Throughout these three periods, one thing remained constant: there was no evidence that the level of drug abuse had changed. Rather, it was the level of media reporting of drug abuse—and, above all, of some dramatic cocaine cases—that soared and plummeted.

The necessary starting point for any evaluation of drug coverage during the summer of 1986 is the unarguable fact that drug abuse is not new in our society. Although any level of drug abuse is a serious social problem, no evidence indicates that the illegal drug culture in the United States is growing. The U.S. National Institute on Drug Abuse (NIDA) has reported that cocaine use has leveled off since 1979. Crack use in 1986 was therefore not a sudden new scourge as viewers were led to believe. Newspapers had been reporting its existence as early as November 1985. Nor is smoking cocaine new: the practice received extensive coverage as long ago as 1980 when actor Richard Pryor was severely burned in an accident that involved free-basing (smoking powdery cocaine). But crack was relatively cheap—and easy to use. The name itself had a memorable, onomatopoeic ring, as if Madison Avenue's top advertising brains had hit upon a catchy new product name. Strictly counting cases, crack usage was a New York City phenomenon with some Miami and Los Angeles cases. For most of the base-line period, cocaine and crack received moderate attention. In March and April 1986, the combined ABC, CBS, and NBC evening newscasts devoted just under 35 minutes to drug-abuse coverage. True, on 28 March, NBC News reported that it had spotted a dangerous new drug threat. "There's a new killer in this country," Roger Mudd reported, "an ultra-strong form of heroin known as Black Tar. . . . It is blamed for a growing number of addicts and corpses." Black Tar heroin is still available on inner-city streets today, but it has seldom made any news.

Why did crack become the big story that summer while Black Tar faded from attention? One reason has to do with those who were affected and where those victims lived. Black Tar stayed in the ghetto, while crack was depicted as moving into "our" neighborhood; that is, the white television viewers' neighborhoods. On 20 March, Rebecca Chase, on ABC's "World News Tonight," reported on Nancy Reagan's visit to public schools in Atlanta as part of her "Just Say No" crusade against drugs. "The use of drugs by students is not new, but the situation is not improving," said

Peter Jennings in introducing the Atlanta story. Chase cited a University of Michigan survey on drug use in high schools: 17 percent of these teenagers were said to use cocaine, "nearly double the rate of 10 years ago." Next, in an interview with a presidential assistant on drug abuse, the rise in cocaine addiction was attributed to crack. But there was "good news" to report as well, Chase said. "The increase in drug education, parental involvement, and treatment ... are all starting to have a real impact."

The good news soon evaporated. Tom Brokaw, on 23 May, began an "NBC Nightly News" special report on crack with these words: "All across America, special police units are cracking down this weekend on a new, highly addictive form of cocaine which is known as crack." Brokaw described arrests in New York's Times Square. Then the report shifted to correspondent Dennis Murphy in Miami. Police are trying to close down "crack houses," he reported. Crack use is out of control. Crack addiction is powerful. "Narcotics officers call it the biggest trouble to hit the streets since heroin. Crack has become America's drug of choice. . . . It's flooding America." The last line was meant to rivet attention, and it succeeded. But was crack really flooding America? Or even the cities shown in the NBC report? Or only parts of those cities? This was not clear. Nor were we told how crack had earned the designation "America's drug of choice." Statistically, alcohol and tobacco were the legal "drugs of choice" in America in the 1980s: 53 million people smoked cigarettes, while 17.6 million Americans were either dependent on alcohol or abused it. Marijuana still ranked as the No. 1 illegal drug. According to the NIDA, 61.9 million people in the United States had experimented with marijuana by the late 1980s.

In June, however, there was indeed a flood: an inundation of cocaine and crack stories in the media. One event, above all, opened the floodgates. On 19 June Len Bias, 22, an All-America basketball star from the University of Maryland, was reported to have died after trying cocaine just once. He was young and black, but no ghetto victim. Two days before his death, Bias had been offered a contract by the Boston Celtics, perennially one of the top teams in professional basketball. The Bias story now had its narrative line: crack had cut short the American dream. Just as Rock Hudson's death served to call national attention to the growing problem of AIDS, Bias's death dramatized the perils of cocaine abuse. Eight days later, another dream was cut short by drugs: a professional football player, Cleveland Browns defensive back Don Rogers, died of a cocaine overdose.

Bias's death had a special effect on opinion makers in Congress and the Reagan administration: he had played for Maryland, a home team in Washington, D.C. From the day of Bias's death until Election Day, Peter Jennings offered to bet his ABC News colleagues, no day would go by without some politician calling for a "crackdown on crack." This prediction was no gamble on Jennings's part. In July alone, there were 74 evening news segments devoted to drugs, some as short as 20 seconds but others more than six minutes long. Total July coverage on the three commercial networks totaled more than two hours, a dramatic increase over the 35 minutes of coverage during all of March and April. Of those two hours in July, almost 53 minutes focused on cocaine and crack. As often happens, the stories became ever more chilling. Television reported that cocaine was claiming younger and younger victims. From college campuses to maternity wards, from addicted adults to addicted infants, images of crack spread across the screen. Tom Brokaw, on 7 July, in an "NBC Nightly News" special segment on cocaine, announced: "It is becoming the college drug of the eighties, replacing marijuana and other substances. . . . about 30 percent of the nation's college students will have tried cocaine before they graduate. . . . an alarming shift." On 11 July ABC's "World News Tonight" reported on babies born with a cocaine addiction from mothers who used the drug during pregnancy.

"These are the newest victims of the American cocaine epidemic," said correspondent John Quinones, as the screen showed crying babies in a nursery. "A helpless generation of newborn infants. They are called cocaine babies because their mothers snorted or smoked cocaine during pregnancy. . . . They can't eat or drink without the help of machines and doctors say they face a life marred by medical problems." Quinones added that in one neonatal unit in Fort Lauderdale, Florida, 20 to 50 percent of the newborns were born to cocaine addicts. The statistic sounded alarming, but we were not told that the figure came from a sample of no more than 100 babies—out of the 3.7 million born in the United States each year. Even one "cocaine baby" is a tragedy, so perhaps it is carping to fret about the need for perspective and to point to the underreporting of infant deaths from lead poisoning, malnutrition, alcoholism, etc.

By the middle of July, the "war" on cocaine and crack had become a part of the forthcoming congressional elections. Congress was nearing its summer break, and as the slow news days of summer sweltered on, the campaigns tried to pick up momentum. Every candidate for senator or representative seemed to have something to say against drugs and just about everyone seemed to get news time to say it. On 28 July ABC's "World News Tonight" did a crack segment that typified the summer coverage. Again there were quick-cut images of SWAT teams bursting into "crack houses" and officials being quoted as saying that New York City has "more crack stops than bus stops." No one challenged the official story, despite the plain lunacy of the "crack stop" line. In late July and August, the cocaine/crack story received another boost, with the highly visual choreography of Operation Blast Furnace. The military operation was promoted as an all-out U.S. attack on cocaine production in Bolivia. Viewers saw American pilots being mobilized to go to South America. Helicopters swooped out of the sky to search out and destroy coca-paste laboratories. Three months later, however, *Newsweek* reported that Operation Blast Furnace had resulted in exactly one arrest. Drug agents later corrected the story: there had been two arrests. Everyone else had been alerted by corrupt Bolivian officials.

In August, television began to turn the cameras on itself. Producers and reporters questioned whether the crack story had been exaggerated, and asked each other if factors of geography could have influenced the story. Does the rest of the country sneeze when there is a cold in New York City, home to the networks, or in Los Angeles, the nation's other media center? "Much of the nation's crack problem is concentrated in New York. Local officials call it an epidemic," Connie Chung reported on NBC on 4 August. "But just how widespread is the crack problem and who is using it?" asked ABC anchor Tom Jarriel on 5 August. Thoughtful journalists began to wonder about choices of words and images, and the whole picture of crack. "It's been called 'drug war summer,'" NBC commentator John Chancellor said on 20 August. In the summer of 1986, he said, "politicians and pollsters rediscovered the national drug problem. . . . But where were all these politicians when the old war on drugs was being lost?"

The storytelling impulse remained strong, and not without reason: on 2 September CBS's "48 Hours on Crack Street" achieved the highest ratings of any CBS news documentary in years, reaching nearly 15 million viewers. The program featured entertainment-style elements: vivid colors, powerful dialogue, emotional sound track. CBS producers made use of charts and statistical data to add perspective. Three days later, NBC aired its own dramatic program, "Cocaine Country." But the statistics on both programs were suspect. "48 Hours on Crack Street" estimated that 5,000 people each day try cocaine and that four million were "current" users in the United States. "Cocaine Country" put the figure at five million "regular" users. It was a "fact" that had not been documented, according to the NIDA; the agency also questioned the 5,000 figure.

Late in the crack summer of 1986, some of my associates asked ABC, CBS, and NBC executives, producers, and reporters who were involved in the superheated coverage what they had learned as they contended with this admittedly complex, explosive, contradictory story. "It's a scary problem," said David DeGiovanni, associate producer of ABC's "World News Tonight." The story itself, he said, "grabs you by the lapels." "We report the news as it exists," declared Timothy Russert, vice-president of NBC News. "It truly was an enormous, active, and breaking story." ABC reporter John Quinones also defended the news system against charges of exaggeration. He did acknowledge that "sometimes we have a tendency to feed on one another, and the story feeds upon itself." One story, however, did not appear to grab television news people by their lapels. On 24 September 1986 the U.S. Drug Enforcement Administration released a report suggesting that all the national attention to crack might have been "excessive." The drug, the agency reported, was a "secondary rather than primary problem in most areas." That night, NBC's Tom Brokaw briefly mentioned the DEA story in his introduction to a report on drug testing for members of the Boston police force. ABC's "World News Tonight" skipped the DEA story. So did the "CBS Evening News with Dan Rather."

Race, Class, and Crime 1: The Brawley Mess

11

In the days before the championship boxing match between Mike Tyson and Leon Spinks in the summer of 1988, a hot rumor swept the East Coast. The Reverend Al Sharpton would be escorting Glenda Brawley, the fugitive mother of Tawana Brawley, from her church sanctuary to ringside in Atlantic City. There, at Trump Plaza, she would take her place among assorted Trumps and stars: Donald, Ivana, Madonna, and Oprah. Much like them, Glenda Brawley, 33, was already something of a media celebrity; indeed, her first name was all that was needed to identify her in tabloid headlines. But this perfect photo opportunity—state troopers pushing past pop culture icons to arrest a defiant mother on pay-TV—was not to be. Al Sharpton, the Reverend Sound Bite, explained why during one of his daily news communiques. The Brawley entourage would not go to Atlantic City, he said, because "we must remain here for the big fight. That's the fight for justice."

The Brawley case, as it has come to be known, commanded the attention of newspapers and broadcast stations in New York and around the country for most of 1988. A legal and media circus featuring charges of rape, racism, and justice denied, the case confused most people from the start. But midway through, well before a New York State grand jury decided that Tawana Brawley's story was a fabrication, the case started to make sense. There was not one Tawana Brawley story, but two: first, the mystery of what had happened to the black girl during the period she was "missing" from her Dutchess County hometown of Wappingers Falls, N.Y., over Thanksgiving 1987; second, the spectacle of Sharpton and lawyers C. Vernon Mason and Alton H. Maddox, Jr.—the Brawley family's advisers—using the case for various purposes, from raising black consciousness to raising cold cash. The themes of the two stories also eventually came into focus. What might be called Brawley 1 was at least in part a teenager's hoax, while Brawley 2 was unquestionably a public fiasco. The grand jury that considered the story of the girl's defilement rejected the teenager's fragmentary early account that she had been held for four days in the woods and raped by a band of white men, one of whom wore a "policelike" badge. The jury's report led those who had followed the case to conclude that Brawley was away from her home for reasons of "a consensual nature," in the words of one person familiar with the case. Brawley 2 became the focus of a second jury, a judicial panel looking into charges that the lawyers Mason and Maddox had knowingly made false statements about the case. The lawyers' suit to block this investigation was rejected by the U.S. Supreme Court in June 1990, and the judicial inquiry lurched forward again.

People's judgments about Brawley 2 really did not depend on another official report. Sharpton borrows from the reputations of Gandhi and Martin Luther King, Jr., wearing a chest medallion with a likeness of the civil rights leader. All three Brawley advisers claim to be trying to change the "racist" American legal system. Their broad case was just: certainly, there is racism in the legal system. But in pressing their cause, the Brawley advisers wrote their scripts as they went along, blustering their way past the facts, and shouting "Fire!" in the crowded street theater of New York—all the while making sure to stay close to the microphones. The great paradox of Brawley 2 was that this dumb show went on for months, encouraged by the authorities and the media. The "white power structure"—as Sharpton calls it—all but propped up the advisers' shaky scenarios. The governor and the attorney general, their eyes on electoral politics as well as the case, gave the appearance of trying to avoid offense to any constituency, black or white. The New York television stations and the city's three tabloids, all locked into tight competition, amplified almost every wild utterance from the Brawley camp. Reporters may have muttered privately about McCarthyite big-lie techniques, but the Brawley family's spokesmen had access to what the media wanted: the story everyone was talking about. "A lot of us were less than vigorous in demanding proof," admits David Diaz, the Channel 4 reporter who filed careful reports on the case from its ugly beginnings.

The Tawana Brawley story—Brawley 1—was essentially a private affair from the start. Tawana Brawley, who was 15 when the events of that Thanksgiving weekend unfolded, had a history of running away from home. Her mother, Glenda Brawley, and the man she lived with, Ralph King, 40, both had a reputation for fast hands. (King served seven years for manslaughter in the death of his first wife.) The *New York Daily News* later reported that Tawana Brawley had sometimes been beaten after staying out all night. In May 1988 reporter Mike Taibbi of WCBS, the CBS-owned station in New York, put on the air witnesses who claimed they had seen her partying during some of the time she claimed she was being brutalized by the white men. Tawana Brawley never provided public details of her abduction. Apparently with the help of her mother, she improvised an alibi for her absence from home. Her advisers insisted, however, that a terrible crime had been committed and that it was being covered up by Dutchess County and New York State authorities.

To the media, the Brawley story had all the elements of lurid crime. When Tawana Brawley was found, some of her hair had been chopped off, she was smeared with dog excrement, and someone had written "KKK" and "Nigger" on her body with a felt-tipped pen. That weekend Glenda Brawley was on the phone to the WCBS newsroom, describing the condition of her daughter. According to Paul Sagan, the WCBS news director, "we all knew there was racism in the U.S., and in the last few years we saw it go beyond discrimination to violence. We were sensitive about the issue, and when we got a call from the Brawley family, we immediately sent out a reporter." Given the "background" of black-white relations in New York, Sagan adds, "We put the story on the air almost automatically, in a way we wouldn't have two years ago." That background included the deaths of Eleanor Bumpurs, Michael Stewart, and in the Howard Beach case victim Michael Griffith. Too often blacks have suffered and died at the hands not just of whites but of white police officers. Tawana Brawley's tale of white rape did not seem implausible. The notion that the police of rural Dutchess County—"crackers," attorney Maddox called them—might be slow to pursue one of their own was not too far-fetched, either. One does not have to be black to hold such thoughts. But those with long memories of black-white relations in America can only shake their heads at the ironies of historical role-reversal: in the Scottsboro Boys case—the sensational sex-race-agitprop story of the thirties—it was a white woman's charge (proved to be false) about a "mob" of black rapists that played to ugly stereotypes.

After the original Brawley rape story was reported, Glenda Brawley received several offers of help. One came from Hazel Dukes, New York State president of the National Association for the Advancement of Colored People. Maddox, Mason, and Sharpton—"activists" who disdain the NAACP as "coon people"—also talked to Glenda Brawley. She decided to make her stand with Sharpton & Co. The new team decided that Tawana Brawley "could not get justice" from Dutchess County and advised her not to cooperate with its investigation. At about the same time, the Dutchess County district attorney, William Grady, took himself out of the investigation, citing "conflicts of interest" (one of the supposed white mob named by the advisers worked for Grady). By January, the advisers began demanding that Governor Mario Cuomo appoint a special prosecutor. There was a semblance of logic in their position. After a mob of young whites attacked three black men in the Howard Beach neighborhood of New York City, Mason had argued that the Queens County district attorney, John Santucci, was not investigating the case with sufficient vigor. Mason held back the testimony of his client, one of the surviving black men, and Cuomo eventually appointed a special prosecutor, Charles Hynes, who won convictions against three of the white youths. As Mason told Ted Koppel on "Nightline," the Brawleys' noncooperation with the initial Dutchess County investigation was "the same strategy that we used effectively in the Howard Beach case. That is, we first cooperated with authorities until they demonstrated that they had no intentions of arresting or prosecuting or investigating the case." Koppel did not pursue it, but the Mason version was not quite the whole story. Cuomo did appoint Hynes, but only after refusing to meet with Mason (who was already busy confounding the system). Instead, Cuomo worked out an agreement with the established black leadership, including David Dinkins, then Manhattan borough president, and Basil Paterson, a former deputy mayor. Still, with the Howard Beach convictions, the confront-the-system strategy got a certain validation.

Brawley 1 developed in a different way. Cuomo met with the Brawley advisers and, in a well-meaning statement, said he wanted the girl treated like one of his own daughters. (The Reverend Jesse Jackson, better briefed, stayed away from the case—and the Brawley advisers—during his campaign in the 1988 New York presidential primary.) In early February Cuomo appointed attorney general Robert Abrams to act as special prosecutor. The supposed "crackers" were off the case; Abrams and his staff of 430 lawyers were on it, to the initial cheers of Sharpton and the lawyers.

In a few days, however, their cheers turned to denunciations. Sharpton eventually likened Abrams to Hitler. Maddox added his own obscenities; Abrams, he suggested, had masturbated over a photo of Tawana Brawley. During late winter and early spring, the advisers' words grew wilder. Sharpton described an Irish Republican Army "link" to the case. "He knew how to speak in perfect sound bites for the evening news," says Mike Taibbi. The I.R.A. connection to Brawley 1 grew out of some idle gossip among reporters killing time; nevertheless, it dominated one Sunday night/Monday morning news cycle.

As the attacks on the "white" criminal justice system grew louder, the system became quieter. Having given the advisers official respectability, Cuomo hung back. Abrams was in a different position. A prosecutor calling witnesses before a grand jury is supposed to proceed in secret and without prejudicing the investigation. Abrams did hint that without the Brawley family's cooperation, the grand jury report would be inconclusive. By April, he seemed willing to produce a low-key document reporting that the girl's story could not be confirmed, and that in the absence of evidence, the case was closed. Later, Cuomo stirred himself and in a public letter urged Abrams to persevere—while continuing to distance the governor's office from the case.

When Maddox and Mason appeared in New York State Supreme Court in Poughkeepsie to oppose the New York grand jury subpoena seeking Glenda Brawley's testimony, the lawyers spoke of "400 years of oppression" of black Americans. Judge Angelo J. Ingrassio responded sympathetically, noting that there was "a great deal of truth" in what the lawyers said. Then Ingrassio sentenced Glenda Brawley to 30 days in jail and a $250 fine for not complying with the grand jury subpoena. Two days later, she took "sanctuary" in the Ebenezer Baptist Church in Flushing. The judge was doing his job, upholding the rule of law. Gandhi's tradition of civil disobedience, which the Brawley advisers claim to follow, also has its rules: when you break "bad" law, you do so with the knowledge that you will be jailed in the course of the struggle to change that law. The Brawley advisers apparently do not oppose grand jury subpoenas in general; in a separate court case, Sharpton himself quite sensibly answered a subpoena rather than risk being jailed. Glenda Brawley's act of defiance was in fact minimally risky. How likely was it that New York authorities would send troopers into a crowded church in front of a dozen television crews? Yet, as street theater, it was marvelously effective. The reporters were back out in force. By June 1988, Brawley 1 seemed headed for a stalemate in which those predisposed to one version or another could glean support for their gut feelings. In reality, though, more than three months before, out of sight of the media and the investigators, Brawley 1 had taken a decisive turn, and Brawley 2 was under way.

Lawyers Maddox and Mason have never made a secret of their strategy of using black criminal cases to put the "white" system on trial. Maddox, who was born in 1945, sometimes sounds as if he wants a separate black nation. Mason, a year younger, has had more modest political ambitions; in 1985 he ran in the Democratic primary for Manhattan district attorney against Robert Morgenthau and won a third of the vote. Sharpton, ten years younger than Maddox, is cut from different cloth: he is a Pentecostal minister without a church, a rock-concert promoter, a youth-movement leader, a sometime informant for the federal government. Each man is intelligent and quick-witted. And each placed his personal cause before Tawana Brawley's. The advisers' priorities have never been more clearly expressed than by a political soul mate, the veteran lawyer William Kunstler, who has used criminal cases as agitprop for decades. Kunstler at the time of the Brawley case represented Larry Davis (charged with the attempted murders of nine New York City police officers) and Darrell Cabey (shot by the subway gunman Bernhard Goetz). Though Kunstler had no connection with the Brawley case, in a 23 June 1988 interview with New York *Newsday*, he seemed to capture its animating spirit. "It makes no difference anymore whether the attack on Tawana happened," Kunstler declared. "If her story was a concoction to prevent her parents from punishing her for staying out all night, that doesn't disguise the fact that a lot of young black women are treated the way she said she was treated. [The advisers] now have an issue with which they can grab headlines."

If Perry McKinnon is to be believed, the advisers made the same argument among themselves. McKinnon, then 39, was the Sharpton associate who broke ranks with the advisers. He said he had known Sharpton for three years. They met at the Brooklyn hospital where McKinnon worked as a security officer and Sharpton kept an office for a letterhead organization known as the National Youth Movement. McKinnon says he had doubts about the Brawley story as early as March; still, he says, he offered to draw on his military service—he is a decorated veteran of Vietnam—and his police work to do some investigating on her behalf. By April, McKinnon concluded that he knew something of what had happened. As he would tell WCBS, "The Tawana Brawley story may be that there is no Tawana Brawley story." McKinnon says he went to Newburgh, 15 miles from Wappingers Falls, and found youths who claimed they had seen Tawana Brawley in the neighborhood at the time of the alleged abduction. McKinnon says he told the advisers about his findings, as he had told them of his previous doubts. According to McKinnon, Maddox told him, "[We] don't need no investigator. . . . I'm not going to pursue it legally, I'm going to pursue it politically." Sharpton was blunter, says McKinnon. In early 1988, Sharpton supposedly said that Tawana Brawley's story "sounded like bull——."

In early May, Mike Taibbi and his producer, Anna Sims-Phillips, traveled the same streets of Newburgh and told Channel

2 viewers essentially the same story that McKinnon says he had told the advisers. Sharpton, however, denounced Channel 2, accused Taibbi and Phillips of fraud, and threatened to sue CBS. In Taibbi's view, that performance cost the advisers McKinnon's loyalty. "He knew our story was true," Taibbi says. McKinnon dropped from sight for a month. On 10 June he called Channel 2. He and Taibbi talked for four hours the following Monday. On Tuesday, they taped a two-hour interview in a suite at the St. Moritz hotel. The Taibbi story was broadcast on Wednesday, the same day a similar story appeared in the *Daily News*. It was written by Richard Pienciak, who had also spent a good deal of time reporting in Dutchess County and getting to know Perry McKinnon. Sharpton dismissed McKinnon as a minor player, "a pathological liar," and "mental," referring to some of McKinnon's reported postcombat psychiatric troubles in the early seventies. Taibbi offered a different view. "Perry was obviously important to the adviser team," Taibbi says. "When we tried to set up interviews with Sharpton to get 'the story,' we dealt with Perry."

During Watergate, reporters on the trail of wrongdoing learned the rule "Follow the money." The tradition of lining one's pockets applies to church as well as state. The coins and bills in the collection baskets passed at the advisers' rallies added up. McKinnon counted $4,300 one Saturday after a Bethany Baptist Church rally, and checks and cash came in the mail from across the country. But money has never been the fundamental point of either Brawley 1 or Brawley 2. It could, of course, eventually trip up the advisers. If they helped solicit funds while knowing that there was no case, they could be charged with mail fraud—another count to go along with the charges of obstruction of justice. A lawyer who counsels clients not to cooperate with a grand jury may find himself afoul of the canon of ethics of the American Bar Association, and so disbarment is still a possibility for Maddox and Mason (though the *New York Law Journal* reported that the executive committee of the New York State Bar Association—the white power structure—has stayed clear of any involvement or statements).

The advisers would have welcomed any of these new lives for the Brawley story. A number of people have wondered why Maddox and Mason first embraced Hynes, the white prosecutor of the Howard Beach case, and then became so angry at him (as they later did with Abrams). They may be mad at Hynes because he *won* the case: with the convictions, there is one less magnet to draw people into the streets. Worse, the system worked. One journalist who has covered the advisers for a number of years suggested to me that a lot of their behavior could be understood if one assumption about the Brawley strategy was made: *they did not want a swift resolution of the case.*

The Brawley lead to follow was not money but the movement, martyrdom—and the media. From the start, the advisers improvised around the basic Tawana Brawley theme. They outsensationalized her own sensational story. The "tests" that disclosed five types of semen in her body, the urine "discovered" in her mouth, the cotton fibers in her nostrils (part of the convoluted I.R.A. "ritual"), the three officials "named" as rapists—all were plucked out of the ozone by the advisers. Then the riffs were played back through the cameras, microphones, and reporters' notepads. The supine media became an accepted part of the entire spectacle. Of a dozen journalists I interviewed for this report, almost everyone fretted about the "overcoverage"—but also found justification for it. The *New York Times*, for example, ran four major multibyline articles that, as a *Times*man says, "established what *didn't* happen." Richard Rosen, city editor of the *Daily News*, holds that because race is such a major issue in the city, allegations of injustice or cover-up deserve the widest attention. Even when the allegations are outrageous? James Hoge, the publisher of Rosen's paper, defends this attention as ultimately useful to the public. "The publicity that demagogues create ends up destroying them," he argues. "They keep raising the ante until they go too far. They become unhinged." The journalistic consensus seems to be that big coverage can serve as an antidote for the big lie.

The public response suggests this may be true. In the winter of 1988, WCBS and the *New York Times* surveyed attitudes about black leadership in the period just before Brawley 1 went off into a more eccentric orbit. Sharpton was found to be the best-known person among black public figures. He also had the highest "unfavorable" rating among blacks, 18 percent. By late June, when a second poll was conducted, Sharpton's unfavorable rating among blacks had tripled, to 58 percent. Eighty percent of whites rated him unfavorable. Further, by large majorities, both blacks and whites said they did not think the Brawley advisers had acted responsibly. Somebody should have told the gatekeepers of the media.

Race, Class, and Crime 2: The Central Park Jogger

12

In 1988, 3,400 rapes and 1,900 murders were reported in New York City. It is one measure of life in urban America today that very few of these rapes and murders "made news." That is, they were not mentioned high up in the local evening newscasts or reported on page 1 of the newspapers for more than a day or two. But the rape of a young woman jogger on 19 April 1989, along the 102nd Street transverse at the north end of Central Park, broke through the usual unremarked routine of death and violence to make headline news all across America.

The story of that night—a clear, cool evening with a full moon riding low over the skyline—became, by every measure, big news. Newspapers in the United States and abroad carried accounts of the "Central Park jogger" and the "wolf pack" that had attacked her. On Monday, 24 April, five days after the assault, the three national networks all ran substantial accounts. The following Sunday, ABC's "This Week with David Brinkley" devoted 45 minutes to the story. *Washington Post* columnist Richard Cohen called for a White House declaration of war, to be led by a task force to "assemble the considerable number of studies already done on the underclass." Dismissing Cohen's "goo-goo experiments," conservative syndicated columnist and television host Patrick Buchanan put forward his own final solution to deal with, in his word, these "savages": if the oldest member was "tried, convicted, and hanged in Central Park by June 1 . . . the park might soon be safe again for women." In a full-page ad in all four New York daily newspapers, real estate developer Donald Trump took up the call for blood vengeance: "Bring Back the Death Penalty. Bring Back Our Police!" he demanded.

What concerned Tom Brokaw, Peter Jennings, Dan Rather, the columnists, and the tycoon was also a topic around office coffee machines and in university classrooms throughout the country. Some people were drawn to the story not because of a Conradian "fascination of the abomination" but out of an obligation to try to make sense of this modern-day heart of darkness. "Watch Channel 7," a journalist friend told me on day 10 of the story, "They have the longest reports." The same day, a young woman exclaimed with some anguish, "As soon as the 'jogger story' comes on, I change channels. I can't bear it."

The case of the jogger and the wolf pack evoked fear, as much about the social contract as about personal safety. But then a powerful obfuscation quickly went to work. The narrative was mangled by the authorities, who presented only selected information about the case, by the press who made (for the most part) honest blunders, and by the Reverend Al Sharpton and company, who barged into the story (and onto the front pages and TV talk shows) once again shouting "Racism!" All of these agents conspired to make the story either something other than it was, or to make something else the story.

The prudent position is to say, "There's a lot about this we don't know. Why they did it, what can be done to prevent such atrocities, etc." Still, there is a lot we do know. Of course, it is a story about crime, punishment, race, class, political posturings, and media excesses. These are familiar, long-standing themes. The twist is that so many of the standard psychosocial explanations and familiar journalistic styles no longer seemed to work. That is one of the reasons why the story commanded attention. What does it mean, for example, to say that the indicted teenagers came from "stable" families or that they were, as a *New York Times* headline put it, "Children of Discipline"? Good students or indifferent ones, they defined themselves by their acts. Moreover, what solace are Americans to take from New York City Parks and Recreation Commissioner Henry J. Stern, who on 28 April announced increased security patrols for Central Park and declared that the park can be made "defendable . . . because it isn't Vietnam"?

A starting point to make sense of this "senseless" crime is for media consumers to remember a cardinal rule of journalism: All Stories Are Not Created Equal. The scene of the crime had its own special resonance: Central Park is an urban archetype. Commissioner Stern called it New York's "front lawn." In recent years it has been partially restored as a place of rest and recreation, as much by private leadership and money as by municipal initiative. But everyone knows that Central Park has not been totally "reclaimed," even as a symbol. The southern part of the park borders on the towers of affluence and culture. The "other park" stretches north toward Harlem and the projects. More important, the victim was not just any victim. She was a symbol of privilege in the city: Wellesley, Yale, Phi Beta Kappa, investment banking, a fast-tracker making her way up, propelled by her admirable energy and intelligence.

The initial newspaper headlines on Friday, 21 April—the police report came too late for the Thursday morning papers—exploded on the pages: "Wolfpack Rapes Jogger" (*New York Post*); "Terror in Central Park: Rape and Rampage" (New York *Newsday*). These first accounts talked about a gang ranging in size from "as many as twelve" involved in the rape (*New York Times*) to "as many as 30" (*Newsday*) responsible for a series of nine attacks all over the north end of the park. By the next day, the story had a fresh headline, a new journalistic "top." Twenty suspects had been questioned, and eight had been charged in the rape. According to chief of detectives Robert Colangelo, some of them had used the term "wilding"—pronounced "wilin' "—to describe their actions. "Wilding," the *New York Daily News* offered, was street slang for "going berserk" or "bugging out." The next day, there was yet another story hook. Manhattan assistant district attorney Elizabeth Lederer, at arraignment proceedings in Criminal Court, told the judge that the suspects had laughed and joked after being questioned by detectives. She said one of the youths had told the police, "It was fun." The *News* took a shortcut: "Wolf Pack Teen Declares: 'It Was Fun,'" a headline eliding the mediating role in the quotation of the assistant D.A.; her advocate's job, after all, was to argue the strongest case for no bail and, later, for a grand jury indictment.

A basic story line had been laid down, one that could be called "The 'No Remorse' Narrative." It did not matter very much that "wolf pack" raids had become, according to a story in the *News* later in the week, commonplace occurrences for shopkeepers around New York City in the past two years. The packs, to be sure, were not after people as much as sneakers and clothing from stores like Herman's and The Gap. The psychiatrist Alvin Poussaint, on ABC News's "This Week with David Brinkley," pushed the pathology back even further, to his own childhood four decades ago in East Harlem. He told interviewer George Will that he had run with a gang back then. "We didn't call it 'wilding,' but we called it 'visiting.'" Visiting did not involve rape or murder, and Poussaint went on to join the Harvard University faculty, writing and teaching about child and family violence. Still, Poussaint said, his East Harlem childhood did involve feelings of "rage." Will, however, wanted to know about the lack of remorse. Poussaint suggested that might be a 14-year-old's way of appearing tough. Nevertheless, the image of callous "savages" was firmly fixed.

The nature of the park attacks and the ages of the accused attackers (from 14 to 17) triggered a collective reaction: they were so vicious, and they were so young. This seemed to be something new. In fact, two rapes were committed in Central Park in the summer of 1984 by a gang of youths led by a 12-year-old. One of the victims, Rosa Tillman, 51, was found raped, battered, and dead next to the 72nd Street boathouse on 22 July. The other victim was left for dead near the boathouse on 24 August. She survived, so her name has not been published. In each case, the news had a short life cycle; both victims were white but they were also homeless women. Perhaps the cases received less attention because the national political conventions and the Olympics were on television at the time. Five years later, it was difficult to find anyone who remembered those cases, until prodded with a few graphic details: one victim had been beaten with a tree limb, the other with a golf club.

In the jogger case, there was further surprise when a portrait of the accused "wildin'" gang began to emerge. The teenagers were described as "middle class." It is instructive to see how the term is defined these days. No drugs appeared to be involved, and no guns were used. All the boys were still in school; "only" one had a police record, and another had only recently started cutting classes. One attended a parochial school where the tuition was $1,100 a year. Most were brought up by their mothers or grandmothers, although two boys, according to the *New York Times*, had fathers who enforced curfews and were "disciplinarians." Four lived in Schomburg Plaza, the high-rise at 110th Street and Fifth Avenue, at the northeast corner of the park. Schomburg, though a city project, is adequately maintained and has an active tenants' association.

The teachers and principals of the accused assured reporters that the boys were "ordinary students" (*Newsday*), "not the kind of kid I would have targeted to be violent" (*New York Times*). Television reporters sought out schoolmates, other teenagers who lived at Schomburg, and basketball players at neighborhood courts to get on-the-street interviews with punchy quotes. Mostly, there was agreement about the accused: the boys wore their hair in flattops or fades; they liked to joke, dance, and play the saxophone; they hung out; they had attitude. These accounts were, in journalistic talk, thumbnail sketches. On the surface, the accused seemed like the teenage boys encountered every day throughout the city. Yet anyone who reads a paper regularly or watches television news will recognize the predictable quotes. Is it really surprising when principals assure visitors that they are in control of their classrooms, doing their jobs well? How often after some horrendous crime, in New York or Texas, big city or small town, have neighbors been quoted as saying, "He seemed like such an average kid?"

The classic line "He was a quiet boy" could be filed for use in 200 cases to come. (Invariably, another "surprise" detonates later, usually involving deep-rooted family pathologies.) Another familiar sound bite comes with a more serious emotional charge, that the case of the Central Park jogger received so much attention because the victim was white. Almost always, it is blacks who advance this argument, mostly in conversations or interviews but increasingly in black-oriented news outlets; in New York such outlets include the *Amsterdam News* and WLIB radio. There are now two versions of reality: one is of mainstream "white" information, not trusted by blacks; the other, a black-based version, dismisses mainstream thinking.

On one level, this represents one more vigorous exercise of First Amendment rights. Station WLIB, for example, offers "community activists" standing access to its talk shows. The *Amsterdam News*, however, used its freedom to print the name of the jogger, becoming the only New York publication to do so. (On television, a Channel 2 reporter blurted out her name during his field report. The station later apologized.) This was a minor matter compared with the performance of the *City Sun*, a weekly paper for the black community with the slogan "Speaking truth to power." A front-page editorial in the 26 April–2 May 1989 issue contrasted the Central Park rape with the Tawana Brawley case. According to the *City Sun*, the white media were "invading the sanctity of [the Brawley] home to show her face," while taking care "to avoid identifying the Central Park woman." What the editorial did not say, although it was widely reported and never contradicted, was that the Brawley family had telephoned the "white media," specifically WCBS-TV, and asked the assignment desk to send a reporter and crew to the Brawley apartment in Wappingers Falls. But the Brawley case had been pure hoax from the start, albeit improvised from week to week. There was no official cover-up reaching as high as New York Governor Mario Cuomo because there was nothing to cover up. The 15-year-old Brawley had run away from home after being hit by her stepfather. She had calculated that the rape story would gain his sympathy and forestall a second beating. She could not have guessed she would become a "cause."

Brawley's charges initially worked as street theater because they had an element of plausibility; her case also had some skilled proponents. As the television journalists Mike Taibbi and Anna Sims-Phillips explained in their book, *Unholy Alliances: Working the Tawana Brawley Story*, the Brawley bunch could not have scammed the city, the state, and, at times, the country without the collaboration of the "white media." "That was the unholy alliance," Taibbi says. "We in the press gave them constant and easy access." The Brawley handlers made a comeback in the jogger case. Lawyer Alton Maddox was an adviser to Joseph Mack, attorney for Michael Briscoe, a 17-year-old indicted for beating a male jogger during the the wildin' night of 19 April (Briscoe was on probation at the time for mugging a teenager five months before). Maddox shouted "Racism!" during Briscoe's court proceedings. Journalism again demonstrated it has no sense of shame. The Reverend Al Sharpton appeared on CNN's "Crossfire" to argue as an "expert" witness in the Central Park case.

Black suspicions of the authorities and the "white media" have not been fashioned out of thin air. The defenders of the young men arrested and later brought to trial for the jogger assault invariably cited police and press behavior in the Stuart case in Boston, another sensational "racial" story. When the police found Charles Stuart wounded and his pregnant wife dying in the couple's car, the husband gave police a description of a black male assailant. The story touched all the modern, urban emotional buttons: vulnerable middle-class whites, predator from the underclass, no one safe in the city no matter how innocent their business (the couple was in the neighborhood for a birthing class). Boston's law enforcement officers and the city's media went on their own wildin' rampage: police rounded up black males around the clock while the papers and television stations cheered them on. Investigators charged off in every direction except the most obvious one (in seven out of ten cases involving a spouse's or companion's murder, the perpetrator is another person in the same household). Finally, Charles Stuart's story fell apart under the weight of its own fabrications, and he stepped off a bridge into a historical footnote: if you kill your wife in Boston, blame a black man—you might get away with it.

The Stuart case keeps black fears alive. But the better parallel to the Central Park case took place in Howard Beach, Queens, where a gang of whites taunted and tried to beat three black men, chasing one onto the Belt Parkway, where he was hit by a car and killed. Howard Beach received major coverage precisely because of race: some of the whites involved were proving their tough-guy standing by claiming "their" territory—atavisms no less "savage" than those of the Central Park blacks. The personal history of their victim was not "the story." He had not gone to Yale or worked on Wall Street; quite the contrary. But that did not diminish the coverage of the case. Many blacks, however, are convinced that social standing determines how much attention a victim receives.

Most rapes get two paragraphs or 15 seconds of coverage. A steady litany of depressing stories—police-blotter news—eventually drives saner members of the audience away. A story about a woman raped and thrown from a rooftop around the time of the jogger case broke through the routine neglect because the narrative had an extraordinary "angle": the victim managed to survive. At the Carver Houses, a few blocks from Schomburg Plaza, three schoolgirls were assaulted on the evenings of 18, 20, and 25 April. Two were raped and sodomized. A neighborhood crack addict known to Carver tenants was sought, but the story never became "big" in itself. The Central Park case put the Carver story on the media map only in a modest way, as a kind of "news by proximity."

Nevertheless, the astute student of the media understands that if the Central Park jogger had been a young black or Hispanic woman with an Ivy League degree and a professional job, the crime would still have been a major news story. The classic narrative themes would have been sounded: achievement blighted, the two faces of the city, is no one safe? The victim would have been "one of ours," part of the middle class. The "white media" are, slowly and somewhat unsteadily, trying to hire nonwhites with similar "good" credentials. Equally important, print and television, and the companies that advertise in newspapers and on television, want these people as readers and viewers. Bluntly, however, the most desirable audience is still largely white. In a moment of truth on the Brinkley program, ABC newsman Sam Donaldson did not so much defend as explain the ways of the media, when he attributed the intensity of coverage to "giving audiences what they want."

The outlook for the news, and for the news audience, proved somewhat worse than the prognosis for the jogger. She made a remarkable recovery, her gallantry combined with the medical skills of her attending caregivers bringing her back to near-normal use of her limbs and neural functions. The trial of her accused attackers turned into a bitter, degraded proceeding, waged as much on the front pages and evening news as in the courtroom. The jogger herself had no memory of the night; 18 months after the attack she still suffered from amnesia and double vision. She needed help to negotiate stairs and often veered to the right or left when walking. No witnesses to the attack came forth during the trial, but there was no shortage of demagogues outside the court, sounding off in hopes of appearing on the evening news.

Romancing the Don

13

Is the dapper don going out of style? There was a full-court press at the trial of John Gotti, the "new Godfather" of the tabloids, the "dark power," as the government called him in its summation one day late in the winter of 1990 in Manhattan Supreme Court in New York City. The television personality Geraldo Rivera tried for an ambush interview, using a hidden tape recorder; John Miller, Barbara Nevins, Pablo Guzman, and the rest of the local evening-news pack jockeyed for position and the favor of a sound bite. The Cable News Network decided to carry the verdict live.

Still, despite the crowds, cameras, and celebrities, the trial had the feeling of a rerun, as if a sated audience were seeing the *Godfather* saga once too often: first the book, then the motion pictures (parts 1, 2, and 3), then the videocassettes. The city's tabloid newspapers, the *Post*, the *News*, and *Newsday* treated the Gotti story modestly, by tabloid standards. The papers and television news shows squeezed what they could out of the hidden tape recordings the government used in its attempt to show that Gotti had ordered the shooting of John F. O'Connor of the carpenters' union. O'Connor himself provided another day's worth of hilarious news; he showed up as a witness for the *defense*, speaking in a voice touched with the brogue and still suffering from a convenient attack of amnesia ("When you see a gun extended toward you, you don't want to look no further").

O'Connor's appearance, and that of one other witness, made up the entire Gotti defense—plus the Gotti lawyers' claim that their client was merely "a salesman for a plumbing contractor" being harassed by a vindictive federal government. The somewhat inept prosecution did not offer much for headline writers, either. Television cameras were permitted in the courtroom, but though CNN bureaus were under standing orders to offer as much live courtroom coverage as possible, the cable network interrupted its all-news format for Gotti only sparingly. By contrast, for the trial of Joel Steinberg in the infamous "little Lisa" case, says a CNN senior producer, "We were there all the time, cutting in and taking it for an hour, depending on who was on the stand."

Around the country, the "new Godfather" story played hardly at all. Howard Kurtz, at the time the New York correspondent for the *Washington Post*, twice tried to interest his editors in Gotti. "My desk's response was lukewarm," Kurtz says. "Gotti is not quite a name beyond the Hudson River." The chief of the *Los Angeles Times*'s New York bureau, John Goldman, eventually filed one major Gotti story. According to Goldman, "Some trials need scene-setters and some need day-to-day coverage; others, like Gotti's, can be treated at the end." This relative inattention to the Godfather saga may be a sign of changing crimes. The *Washington Post*'s newsdesk "had a few other things to worry about, like the troubles of [Mayor] Marion Barry," says Kurtz. Once, gangland-style rubouts intrigued readers. Middle America absorbed Cosa Nostra lore; it learned the difference between *capos* and *consiglieri* and was aware of what terms like *zecchinetta* and *comare* meant. Today the popular imagination fixes on white-collar criminals on Wall Street. The trails and travails of Leona Helmsley, Ivan Boesky, and Michael Milken all played very well. "Leona was huge in Washington," says Kurtz. "She became a symbol of greed in the eighties."

Perverse as it sounds, organized crime's bad deeds now seem relatively bloodless and remote from everyday concerns. Younger women, in particular, appear uninterested, as if the mob were a minor league team mentioned in small type on the sports pages. "There was no emotion at the Gotti trial," says one woman, an executive producer at one of the networks, who had been closely involved in coverage of the story. On the other hand, "The Joel Steinberg case had incredible drama: little dead Lisa, the battered woman on the stand, the issue of child abuse." Similarly, in the Howard Beach trial, this producer says, "We had to confront personal matters, like racism in ourselves and in society." But no one was killed in the Gotti case, and there was no recognizably decent soul to empathize with: just rival groups of goons hitting on one another. Even the economic costs to society of the mob's operations—from bookmaking, boosting goods at JFK International Airport, labor racketeering, skimming of legitimate businesses—go largely unremarked. People usually fail to relate organized crime to their daily lives; they treat it as if it existed only up there on the screen and not down here in reality.

The Godfather story had a long run. For decades, journalists knew that there were two institutions about which they could unleash their imaginations: the mob and the politburo. Both conducted their work in secret, without press releases or background-briefing papers. Journalistic speculation about their inner power struggles and strategies was not likely to produce a letter to the editor demanding corrections or amplifications. Once Mikhail Gorbachev threw open the Kremlin's doors, the mob seemed to be the sole safe preserve for such creative writing. Moreover, the mob story took on new life with the appearance of John Gotti—compact, confident, steady-eyed, the first celebrity gangster since Frank Costello. In his bespoke suits, hand-painted silk ties, and diamond pinkie ring, Gotti seemed custom-made for television and the tabloids. "We needed him," argues John Miller, who covers crime and police news for WNBC television in New York. The aging dons of the generation that Gotti replaced were usually turkey-necked and stooped, candidates for nursing homes rather than the evening news. "These frail old guys stumbled around in suits that didn't fit," says Miller. "We'd see them and then go to the movies and see something better, like Michael Corleone. Young, smooth, what the new Godfather should look like." Then came Gotti, and Miller and his cross-channel rivals on the crime beat finally got the don they deserved, one who looked like the Hollywood version.

The new narrative line starring Gotti worked well until the trial in Manhattan Supreme Court. Gotti initially presented the image reporters and editors appreciate. "He wanted to be noticed. You were being handed a colorful picture," says an assignment editor. "Just look at those monogrammed Gucci socks," adds John Goldman. "I think Gotti went to the same movies we did," says John Miller. Gotti then made a bad career move. Not content with swaggering through the press pack waiting for him between the fifth-floor courtroom and his chauffeured car outside on Centre Street, he began feeding sound bites to the newshounds. He did not put on his earphones to monitor the prosecution's tape recordings, he told Pablo Guzman of Channel 5 and Mary Murphy of Channel 2, because he likes to listen instead to Julio Iglesias, the Latin-Pop singer (where were Verdi and Puccini when the media needed them?). When John Miller asked Gotti how his day in court had gone, the dapper don's devastatingly witty comeback was "How was yours?" After the courtroom summations featuring bitter exchanges between the defense and prosecution attorneys, Gotti told reporters that his man, the burly lawyer Bruce Cutler, "shoulda hit (the other guy) in the chin."

The courtroom tapes offered further brackish thoughts from the shallows of Gotti's mind. The 49-year-old man in the $2,000 suit came across like an eighth-grade dropout. No surprise there: he is. The government-supplied transcripts, with their "f———" and "s———," did not knock anyone's Gucci socks off, either. Nixon's

White House tapes long ago prepared courtroom eavesdroppers for boys' locker-room talk like Gotti's. But the movie-fed mythologies about the mob—love and respect for the family, for instance—really took it on the chin when certain tapes were played. In one conversation, the government's transcript revealed Gotti dismissing the possibility of a specific turn of events involving the carpenters' union: that was as unlikely, the don supposedly says, "as my mother [having sex with] Reagan."

Once Gotti opened his mouth to speak, he undercut the silken image. He was like a silent-screen star felled by the arrival of the talkies. His words are not likely to live on in the popular mind; as sound bites, they do not compare to Leona Helmsley's "Only the little people pay taxes." Worse, the whole dapper don image may have become hopelessly downscale for contemporary tastes. Well before the case went to the jury, the *Daily News* delivered a verdict on Gotti. A reporter from the paper, Mark Kriegel, went to Barneys and other up-market clothiers for comment on Gotti's habit of wearing matching sets of ties and pocket squares. They are frowned upon, Kriegel was told: they look "cheap" and "forced."

Terrorvision: Taking the Camera Hostage

14

"The terrorists won, right?" ABC News correspondent Sam Donaldson pressed a Reagan administration official on the day in June 1985 when 39 hostages from TWA Flight 847 were freed.

In the competitive atmosphere of American television coverage of hijackings and hostage takings, a strange mutant form of news treatment has taken hold, one that might be called terrorvision. Donaldson's statement phrased as a question seemed to be the perfectly understandable expression of this form. Television news gave such dramatic, blow-by-blow attention to the hijacking, it was only natural that, in television's hands, the story became a kind of deadly game; there were obvious winners, and by Donaldson's implication, apparent losers, such as Ronald Reagan, the United States, Israel, and Western ideas about the rule of law. A careful review of the coverage, however, shows that one clear-cut loser may have been television itself.

The review embraced the news output of four U.S. networks over the 17-day period between the start of the TWA 847 hijacking on 14 June 1985 and the hostages' release on 30 June—an exhaustive record of some 60 hours of television that included materials ranging from two-minute bulletins to hour-long special programming. Television news people did much that they could be proud of: there were individual examples of hard-working anchors, physically courageous field reporters, incisive commentators, and concerned producers, as well as feats of technical wizardry. But when the parts were added up, the television system collectively went wrong. It was as if the too-potent mixture of competitive zeal and Mideast politics transformed moderate television into extremist terrorvision, Dr. Jekyll into Mr. Hyde. Thus, while ABC commentator George Will was decrying the "pornography of grief" on the screen, ABC and its competitors were piling on the scenes of anxious hostages and their anguished families. This schizophrenic pattern of individual journalistic achievement and collective news mindlessness can best be traced by seeing the story—with the benefit of hindsight—as a melodrama in three acts: the hijacking event, the hostage crisis, and the political resolution.

The Event The first impression a viewer gets when replaying the videotapes of the television coverage is one of the news strength of ABC, CBS, and NBC—and, to a lesser extent, CNN. These organizations assembled the piece of the story with speed and competence. On 14 June, Day 1 of the hijacking, for example, CBS offered special coverage on "CBS Morning News," "CBS Evening News," and "Newsbreak," plus 10 special reports, ranging from one to six minutes, during the broadcast day, and a 30-minute news special at 11:30 P.M. The other networks were equally impressive covering the breaking news. NBC had nine special reports totaling 38 minutes and 42 seconds on Day 1, plus coverage during its regular news programs. The networks' evening newscasts quickly touched on all aspects of the story: the initial hijacking after flight 847 left Athens, the first landing at Beirut airport, the next leg to Algiers, and the return to Beirut, which, astoundingly, took place while the evening newscasts were on the air. ABC's "World News Tonight" that evening was typical of the "routine" special performances the networks can mount. There were reports from London, from the State Department, and from a terrorist "expert" with a Washington think tank. Next, Peter Jennings interviewed

Israel's ambassador to the United Nations. Then, from around the country, came the longest segment: emotion-laden interviews with family members and friends of the Americans aboard the plane. These interviews would be one of the signatures of television news coverage during the next two and a half weeks. The most dramatic segment was an audio clip that all three network evening news programs used at the beginning of their reports, the voice of TWA pilot John Testrake beseeching the Beirut control tower to let him land and refuel: "They are beating the passengers! . . . They are threatening to kill them now! . . . We want the fuel now!"

Analysts often speak of "the fog of war," that is, the near-chaos of extended military engagements that make reliable accounts difficult to achieve. A similar cloud envelops long-running hostage stories. There was considerable confusion at the start about whether the passengers with "Jewish-sounding names" were singled out (by passport inspection) and removed by the Shiite gunmen to be kept apart from the other Americans. This "Jewish list" varied; the network accounts, quoting TWA spokesmen and other sources, varied from 6 to 12 names. After all the hostages were freed, the true situation emerged. American males who were without U.S. passports or who had a "military look"—for example, the U.S. Navy man Robert Stethem—were special targets of the terrorists. While Stethem was murdered, another military man, Claude Whitmoyer, went unharmed. Whitmoyer held a top-secret clearance and worked with a U.S. national security agency, information that at least two networks knew and withheld. Reporters also knew more than they told about the movements of the U.S. antiterrorist military unit, the Delta Force, although they did report sketchy information about the size, general destination—and practical uselessness—of the unit.

The Crisis Individual reporters and newsdesks behaved with restraint and sensitivity to strictly military matters in the early days of the coverage. But other systemic forces drove the coverage more and more toward terrorvision, and effectively limited the Reagan administration's political options. The first factor was the superheated air of crisis that filled the screen. On Day 2, CBS broadcast 13 special reports in addition to its scheduled reports and expanded coverage on the Saturday evening news. On Day 3, CBS had 17 special reports in addition to its scheduled newscasts. Dan Rather was never more than a few moments away from the viewer that weekend, nor was Peter Jennings at ABC. Tom Brokaw cut short a family vacation on safari in Africa and flew to Beirut for NBC.

The presence of these important media figures morning, noon, and night signaled the importance of the hostage story. The networks' magazine programs and their morning shows also joined in. "CBS Morning News" scrapped its usual format to become a Hostage Central, with reporters Bob Schieffer and Terence Smith. The ABC late-night program "Nightline," which began during the Iranian hostage-taking in 1979, has since become a fixture of crisis journalism. The program discussed the TWA hijacking every night for two weeks. Ted Koppel rounded up the usual terrorism experts, including the same faces that appeared earlier in the evening, as well as Mideast diplomats and the ubiquitous Henry Kissinger. On the network evening shows, almost 60 percent of air time in the period from 14 June to 30 June was devoted to the hostages and related stories, as if nothing else remotely as important was happening in the United States or the world. In between regularly scheduled newscasts, short bulletins during station breaks continued to stoke the crisis feeling: "Are positions hardening? Details later tonight," they promised. Broadcast journalists, tellingly, call these materials "teases." On CNN, the normal rotation of the anchor teams gave a more matter-of-fact demeanor to the story. Still, CNN added its own melodrama by periodically scrolling down the screen the list of the names of hostages.

In part, all this exciting buildup and portentous delivery reflected the sensible news judgment that this was indeed a big story. In part, though, the excitement reflected less sensible competitive pressures to be first with the most. It signified that news organizations have the technical resources to pull a big story together and create a momentum even when nothing may be happening. These resources were used to sustain a moment-to-moment crisis feeling, which in turn took some policy initiatives away from Reagan administration decision makers. The networks, rather than Washington, controlled the public level of interest in the story. The Reagan White House tried at first, for example, to hold down coverage; later it acknowledged its inability to do so. But then the networks began to lose their own control over the story to two other entities. One was the terrorists' stand-ins, the Amal militia; the other was the hostages' surrogates, their families and supporters.

This shift in control occurred because both the hostage-takers and the hostage-sufferers could provide the good pictures that the television system wanted. Serious journalists, like ABC anchor Peter Jennings and Roone Arledge, the president of ABC News, may wince in private about the often maudlin pictures of husbands and fathers expressing their desires for freedom, and wives and children reciprocating the anguish, yet the images were riveting. The home viewer predictably responded: "Those folks could be the people next door. They could be me!" The scenes were "good television"—and ABC and their rivals are in the business of doing good TV. Once television fleshed out the terse bulletins with human faces and endowed the crisis with everyday emotions, Delta Force and all the other military alternatives thought to be available to the administration ceased to exist as practical options. As CBS White House correspondent Lesley Stahl explained on "CBS Morning News": "We [the television networks] are an instrument for the hostages. . . . We force the administration to put their lives above policy." The hostage families realized this truth. Many made themselves available to every talk show and interviewer that came their way, "to keep public awareness as high as we can," as the brother of one hostage told the *Boston Globe*. Conventional wisdom holds that television arrogantly besieges hostage families. That may have been so in the past; today, in a media-savvy society, desperate families can take hostage a compliant television system.

The other controllers of the television system, of course, were the Shiite Moslem terrorists and their Amal militia allies. It is a cliché now to point out that the Shiite faction manipulated American journalists to carry its political message back to the United States. When the television coverage is replayed on a VCR, a viewer can see just how well the Shiite line was delivered. The original terrorists murdered an American citizen, Robert Stethem, and beat others. Their "moderate" accomplices later robbed passengers of money and jewelry. It is still shocking, even in retrospect, to see how quickly the coverage moved on from this thuggery, although Dan Rather, to his and CBS's credit, got angry enough on camera to rail about how the terrorists took "somebody's son . . . beat the hell out of him and shot him to death." Mostly, however, the television system maintained a collective calm and "objectivity." On ABC's "World News Tonight" on 21 June, Don Kladstrup reported on the Shiite Moslems, describing them as "the losers in life, the people who've been pushed from their homes in the South." Kladstrup interviewed an older man who, the audience was told, had two sons in an Israeli prison. "I sympathize with American families," this father said. "My sons are hostages, too." Holding to its "objectivity," television was able to strike a kind of moral equivalence that made the kidnapping of 39 Americans who happened to be on an Athens-to-Rome flight the same as the removal to Israel of a group of Shiite Moslems detained by Israeli troops during their occupation of Southern Lebanon. On 27 June ABC News correspondent Charles Glass had an exclusive interview—arranged by Amal—with three hostages, including Allyn Conwell, who was an oil company salesman based in Oman.

Conwell referred to the Israeli-held prisoners as "hostages" and spoke of his "profound sympathy" for the Amal cause. Such "objective" reporting can create a fog of its own. Fortunately, ABC commentator George Will cut through the murk. He called the Kladstrup report "heart-rending," but added that it was of little practical relevance: "If you're confronted on the streets of Manhattan with an armed fanatic, the problem is not to cure him; it's to cope with him."

During this crisis phase, ABC gave more time to the hostage story than the other networks (all-news CNN excepted). ABC also had more exclusive interviews with selected hostages. ABC obtained these interviews for good journalistic reasons: it had people on the ground in Beirut, notably Glass and Julie Flint, who, during the earlier agonies of the Lebanese civil war, had developed excellent contacts with the various political factions. The ABC people had in-country experience, the kind that journalism's critics are always urging news organizations to develop in their reporters. Among other firsts, Glass was able to approach the hijacked TWA plane on Day 6 and get an interview with Captain Testrake. Both *Time* and *Newsweek* put on their covers the picture showing Testrake with a gun at his head—the defining image from that interview. Glass also did the long "sympathy" interview with Conwell (and two other hostages) and, working with ABC producer Derwin Johnson, recorded the extraordinary "dinner by the sea" on 28 June. There, at Beirut's Summerland resort hotel, 14 hostages were seen dining with their Amal militia guards, including one described by Peter Jennings as "security chief Akif Haidar, who himself hijacked a Libyan airliner six years ago."

There was a surreal nature to some of the footage; on one occasion, hostage Simon Grossmayer, held at Amal headquarters, took a phone call from genial David Hartman, host of "Good Morning America," back in ABC's studios in Washington. This led to some disparaging remarks about ABC standing for the Amal

Broadcasting Company. The charge was unwarranted but deserves exploration for what it tells us about terrorvision and the muddled new world of media. ABC has treated the Lebanese Moslems in a different way than CBS or NBC. On 24 June, Day 11, all three evening news shows played the tape of an interview Amal conducted with eight hostages:

ABC's Peter Jennings: "Good evening. We have another opportunity today to see some of the hostages in Beirut. The videotape was made by a Lebanese cameraman working for a British news agency and made available to all the American networks."

CBS's Dan Rather (voice-over): "Videotape made and released by their captors. Good evening . . . The Shiite Moslem kidnappers released the latest videotape of their victims." *CBS Correspondent Bill Redeker*: "These scenes recorded three days ago by Amal . . . the tape has been edited by Amal."

NBC's Roger Mudd: "Good evening . . . The most dramatic information out of Beirut came in a series of brief interviews with eight of the TWA hostages. The hostages volunteered almost no information. They were questioned by a member of the Amal. In the room at the time, but not seen in the pictures, are the Amal militia. The recording was done Thursday by a Visnews crew and held by the Amal until it was released tonight to the American networks."

The Day 11 story can serve as a journalism-textbook case: the same picture, yet three sharply different captions. In ABC's "soft" account, the name Amal never appears. In Dan Rather's hard-nosed lead, tough words explode from the screen: captors, kidnappers, victims. On NBC, Mudd's narration is neutral, more "factual." Not so incidentally, all three versions are true; like the blind men touching and describing the elephant, each account emphasized a different aspect of reality. But whether the narration took a hard or a soft line, each network used the tape in full. Much like the hostages' families, the Shiite Moslems had grasped the lure of the picture: America, here are your husbands, sons, fathers—safe, so far. Give in so you can have them back.

Resolution and Reaction During the crisis phase, the boisterous behavior of some camera people and microphone-toting reporters forced the temporary postponement of one Amal-sponsored news conference—a "media circus," Roger Mudd called it on NBC that evening. While he was perhaps expressing the general feeling, less disdain and more realism were required. The journalists on the ground were following implicit orders; if they missed the good picture or the telling quote, the desk editors back at New York headquarters would have sent what the news trade calls a rocket: "Where ours, pls?" The real circus behavior involved such home-office habits as flying families overseas and arranging hotel rooms for teary reunions—for the benefit of the cameras. The "Today" show has been a major offender in this regard, apparently unconcerned that its practice of paying for its news sources/guests is closer to entertainment-show policies than to news operations. Another questionable practice of the terrorvision form has to do with live, unedited interviews. The audience sees a news conference as it happens, the story in the making. CNN, without the time constraints of the others, can let its cameras roll. In some of these situations, CNN triumphed; for example, with its news conference centering on the heroic TWA stewardess Uli Derickson. The sappiest use of live television, however, came from people who should know better. David Hartman on "Good Morning America" concluded a live interview with Nabih Berri on Day 15 by earnestly asking the Amal militia leader: "Any final words to President Reagan this morning?" It was exactly the kind of dumb political matchmaking that has led to long-standing complaints about "television diplomacy." Significantly, ABC's "World News Tonight" never used any live, unedited interviews with news sources, and Peter Jennings sought to distance himself from what the "entertainment part of the company" did on the Hartman show. Viewers, though, do not make all that many distinctions between a morning-show host and an evening-news anchor.

By the end of the TWA 847 story, the television system was showing a capacity for self-examination of its role as a facilitator of events rather than their mere recorder. With the hostages' safety assured, television became a hall of mirrors; from dawn on the morning news until late evening on "Nightline," experts looked at the role of television looking at the hostage story (as this analysis does, holding up yet another mirror). With the hostages home, and the dead buried, everything seemed to return to "normal." But as viewers resumed their summer ways, the issue of network culpability, or at least complicity, remained to be admitted. Some Reagan administration officials, including the attorney general of the United States, suggested that television news consider delaying some reports of terrorist activity. Whenever officials send such messages, broadcasters feel obliged to denounce government control. But the choice is not really between Chinese-style nonnews and the present headless system. As one of the numerous specialists on terrorism pointed out on "World News Tonight" during the TWA 847 crisis, everyone around the world knows American television's "great reputation for putting on anything that moves." Or, if network executives need a voice from their own ranks, they might look again at John Chancellor's commentary on "NBC Nightly News" on Day 12: "The fanatics want America in agony," Chancellor said. "They want public displays of grief, America brought to its knees. . . . Let's not play into their hands."

So true, and yet does anyone dare to imagine that the terrorvision scenario will be abandoned from hijacking crisis to hijacking crisis in the years ahead?

Seeing Red: Images of the USSR

15

"How Reckless Are the Russians?" the cover of *U.S. News and World Report* asked. Inside, the magazine offered its account of the nuclear reactor disaster at Chernobyl in the Soviet Ukraine in April 1985. The magazine's question, note well, was not "Are the Russians reckless?" in their operation of nuclear plants, or even "How reckless is the use of nuclear power?" The issue was settled; a closed, dictatorial society such as the Soviet Union can be expected to take chances with the health and safety of its population. Moreover, not only were the Soviet authorities careless about ordinary people in the workers' socialist society; they could also be counted on to cover up, to stonewall. There had to be more than the two deaths announced in the early Soviet accounts, U.S. secretary of state George P. Shultz immediately declared, without citing the basis for his statement. Because the Soviets are masters of deceit, Shultz did not have to elaborate on his statement, any more than *U.S. News and World Report* had to expand on its Chernobyl analysis. As Americans and as American media consumers, we knew the Russians were not to be trusted. (Later, the Soviets put the official death toll at 31; in addition, because as many as 600,000 people in the Ukraine and Byelorussia received significant exposure to radiation, estimates of eventual cancer deaths from the Chernobyl accident range from 10,000 to 100,000.)

The Chernobyl disaster shook up those of us who try to make sense of how we know what we know. The formal name for this effort at understanding is "epistemology"; applied to media, epistomological analysis examines what the press tells us (the news of the day) and how it conveys this information (the techniques of news coverage). This pursuit may seem abstract when dealing with Chernobyl, especially considering more immediate worries, such as the worldwide consequences of radioactive fallout (Should I give my infant iodine extract?) and the overall safety record of nuclear power plants (Should I panic about the plant near where I live?). Tragic long-term radiation effects on children in the Ukraine are still being felt. But the fallout from ideas, from what we think we know and from what we "know" that is actually wrong, can also be dangerous. This is true not just for the ideas conveyed by the daily "hard" news; it is also true for the themes expressed in our popular culture through such diverse sources as the television commercials for Wendy's and Midas Muffler and the *Rocky* and *Rambo* movies of Sylvester Stallone. As the Chernobyl story developed, the Soviets received a pummeling at the hands of American news organizations, somewhat like Rocky's Russian opponent Ivan Drago. Much of this treatment was deserved, given the performance of important actors in the USSR. Nevertheless, the American media record is hardly unblemished; its performance reveals how popular images are formed, and also the relationship of news organizations and the image industries to government and foreign policy.

From the start of the disaster, the Soviets were less than forthcoming. The authorities were infuriatingly slow in alerting their near neighbors, such as Poland and Sweden, to the accident. The details that were supplied were scant—more bland reassurance than usable facts. For Americans with good memories, the pattern should have been familiar. Seven years before Chernobyl, they had lived through the accident at Three Mile Island, site of the nuclear power plant operated by Metropolitan Edison of Pennsylvania. Then, too, a company spokesman had attempted to minimize what had happened and to accent the positive, "contained" nature of the event. There was some minor damage, he had said, as well as the release of "very small traces" of radioactivity; but overall the system had worked and shut itself off. The first Three Mile Island story was presented reassuringly, with the accident already referred to in the past tense. Of course, it was not over; the problem immediately got worse worse. Later, we learned how enormous confusion within the plant combined with bureaucratic bumbling and the "normal" defensive posture at all levels of large organizations (the strategy of "cover your ass") to minimize the danger. Joseph Hendrie, then head of the federal Nuclear Regulatory Commission, likened himself and the Pennsylvania governor at the time, Dick Thornburgh, to "a couple of blind men stumbling around making decisions." At Chernobyl, too, we can infer from more recent Soviet statements, the on-site officials sought to minimize the accident and keep their superiors in the dark. This context helps to explain why Soviet officials initially announced that "only" two people had died in the explosion and fire. It is the nature of radiation to kill over a period of days and weeks. The Soviets' first words probably were true, though bureaucratically slippery.

If bureaucrats, East and West, instinctively behave the same way, then where did the images of "reckless" Soviets and uncaring Kremlin masters come from? In large part, they already existed in our minds. More than 70 years ago, the political analyst Walter Lippmann spoke of "the pictures in our heads": images about events, people, and places we know secondhand, from the press, from our education, and from the authorities. We have such pictures of the Soviets, as we do of Chinese, Ugandans, Israelis, Nicaraguans, and anyone else we have given some thought to but have not actually met. Sometimes, these images of what "everyone knows" are accurate. In the case of the Soviet Union, most everyone would agree that, say, Siberia has cold winters; that the czarist economy missed out on part of the Industrial Revolution; that Stalin was a monster who caused unparalleled suffering; and that Soviet leaders have been isolated, secretive, and suspicious. There are some enduring truths, but perhaps not as many as we might guess and maybe not the ones we would expect. A look at the manner in which the Soviet Union has been presented in the American media and in American popular culture during two contrasting periods produces some provocative results. The periods of contrast selected were the early 1970s, in particular the time of President Richard Nixon's trip to Moscow, in May 1972, for a summit meeting with Soviet leader Leonid Brezhnev, and the mid-1980s, around the time of President Reagan's trip to Geneva for his summit meeting with Mikhail Gorbachev in November 1985.

Twenty years ago, America was very much aware of the Soviet Union as a powerful political adversary. Americans believed that the USSR had achieved military parity with the United States; some contended that the Soviet Union was ahead in certain aspects of nuclear weaponry. Then, as now, politicians and press monitored the Soviet Union, noting, for instance, its alliances with China and its overtures to European countries. In a story that appeared at the time of Nixon's 1972 meeting with Brezhnev, *Newsweek* reported no signs that the Soviets were abandoning designs to expand their influence around the world. Throughout the 1970s the American media continued to probe these global motives. *Time* magazine, in its 22 May 1972 issue, ran a long article entitled "Why the Russians Do What They Do." The report explored the USSR's abiding fear of China, its concerns for detente, and its need to find economic policies that would suit its self-interest. In these and other accounts, coverage of the Soviet Union during the Nixon era was cautious and wary. No one could accuse Nixon or his administration of being soft on the Soviets. But it was Nixon's policy to relax great power tensions, and print and broadcast stories followed his lead by discussing aspects of Soviet life with a certain benevolence. There was no automatic blaming of the Communist system for social and economic privations. There were attempts, albeit somewhat condescending, to draw comparisons between the Soviet way of life and an America of past decades. For example, a *Chicago Tribune* reporter told his readers in June 1972, right after Nixon's Moscow visit, about the Soviet people's robust spirit: "At a dance, they reminded me of the farm girls in Iowa. The whole place reminded me of a Friday night in Iowa years ago, where the working people drank plenty, cut loose with loud talk and singing. Earthy is the right word." Similarly, "Russia," a 1972 television documentary, portrayed the Soviets as "not unlike us." "Soviet people feel very close to the American people despite being bombarded with daily propaganda against us," commented producer-director Theodore Holcomb. "What almost any one of them will tell you is that what they really want is a small piece of land with a home on it. Now isn't that the American dream of a few decades ago?" Discussing the Soviet underground comic strip "Octobriana," whose heroine combats evil and yearns for the true revolution that would solve political and social problems, the *Chicago Tribune* asked, "Are these not curiously, rather touchingly, similar to efforts in the West?" In the same spirit, Soviet attention to physical fitness was related to an American context. According to a *New York Times* report of 27 February 1972, "The jogging fad, delayed by the cultural lag that separates the Soviet Union from the West, is just beginning to catch on here, with some fitness buffs running around the block in the morning before setting off for work." The emerging portrait is one of a rather sad life-style, characterized by deprivations.

No 1972 news story or documentary, however, reached for the emotional "hot button" of the American psyche quite like the

"Tanya" political commercial that Richard Nixon's reelection committee used in the fall presidential campaign. Nixon's Democratic party opponent, George McGovern, sought to frame the campaign issues by recalling Nixon's years as a hardline anti-Communist, longtime cold war warrior, and defender of the Vietnam War. To counter McGovern, the Nixon people made a campaign commercial using TV news footage of Nixon's visit to a Leningrad cemetery to commemorate those who had died during the city's heroic resistance to German armies during World War II. The Nixon spot showed the faded black-and-white photo of a 12-year-old girl, named Tanya, with the haunting face of an Anne Frank; Nixon's voice is heard, declaring, "The pages of her dairy tell the terrible story of war. . . . finally the last words of her diary: 'All are dead. Only Tanya is left.'" Then Nixon himself appears on camera: "As we work toward a more peaceful world, let us think of Tanya and of the other Tanyas and their brothers and sisters everywhere." Cut to photograph of Nixon with his campaign slogan, "Now more than ever. Nixon."

If "Tanya" serves as a dominant image of the Soviets in the period of Nixon detente, then the "Bear in the Woods" can stand as an image for the militant Reagan years. The "Bear" appeared in 1984 as part of Reagan's reelection campaign. Like "Tanya," it, too, was a televised political spot that reached out and touched deep emotions. The spot began with a long distance picture of a brown bear lumbering through the woods. The voice of Hal Riney, consummate advertising executive and creative talent (the Gallo Wine commercials, the Michael Jackson video for Pepsi Cola) intones how we must be careful of the bear, that it can be dangerous, and how important it is to be prepared. Finally, in the distance, the viewer can glimpse a tall, lean hunter, a Gary Cooper figure, or perhaps Ronald Reagan, alert and on guard. Then comes the sponsor's message: Reelect President Reagan. So different from "Tanya" in content, the "Bear" belongs nevertheless to the same popular art form and has the same overall aim: vote for me, because I know how to deal with the Soviets and the world.

Reagan's political career, like Nixon's, began during the cold war years, and he shared Nixon's hyperawareness of the competition between East and West. But Reagan's rhetoric changed, and so did the discourse of the media. Stories still drew comparisons between the Soviets and the Americans, but the stories recast the Soviets: they were no longer Grant Wood figures trying to catch up to the United States. Reagan spoke of the Soviet "evil empire." Journalism, while still recognizing the Nixonian notion of a rough U.S.-Soviet strategic parity, came down hard on the Soviet government as the source of its peoples' economic and social woes. Victims of Soviet propaganda, Soviet citizens were regarded as beyond help, easily molded clay in the hands of a controlling education and media system. At the same time, there was a growing Western confidence that the lure of capitalist culture would succeed in lifting the blinders that obscured the Russians' view of what they "really" wanted. Thus Richard Threlkeld, reporting from Moscow for ABC's "World News Tonight," during the second Reagan administration, found that despite propaganda efforts to portray America as corrupt, the Soviet people somehow retained good feelings about Americans: "Apparently one of so many things made in Moscow that doesn't work quite the way it's supposed to is the propaganda machine."

In September 1985, right before the Reagan-Gorbachev summit, the *New York Times* coverage of the Moscow Book Fair repeatedly referred to a Soviet "hunger" for details of U.S. life: "forbidden fruit to hungry patrons." An editorial in the *Times* quoted an unnamed Russian woman who stood in line at the fair: "We wait like this for food, and we wait like this for knowledge." They also hankered, in the news accounts, for the artifacts of popular American culture: jeans, rock and roll, soft drinks. Western vigor was contrasted with the lumpish Soviets, whose emotional ups and downs are tied to the length of a food line. CBS correspondent

Mark Phillips, reporting from Moscow, offered a background report on the Soviet Union during the Geneva summit for the "CBS Evening News." Phillips (on camera): "The Soviets have turned a life-style of doing without into a science.... The massive investments Soviets have had to make in their military to match U.S. investments has taken its toll on domestic economy." In a similar background report that same week, Garrick Utley reported on the "NBC Nightly News": "Sixty-eight years after Bolsheviks stormed the Winter Palace . . . there's not much to celebrate." Consumer goods are only one of the necessities that the Soviets must do without. ABC's "World News Tonight" for 1 February 1986 reported, "Their traditions are older, their memories longer than ours, but the sturdy, long-suffering Russian peasants missed out on some things, like the Renaissance, the Reformation, and the Magna Carta." Russian culture was portrayed as frozen, moribund; even the weather conspires to prevent progress. The *New York Times*'s correspondent Philip Taubman, describing a Moscow park during Indian summer, compares it to New York's Central Park but notes that while foreign tourists go around in short sleeves, the Soviets are bundled up: "Once committed to winter . . . Muscovites were unwilling to turn back, or, at least unwilling to unpack the light clothes that won't reappear until the late spring." Tom Fenton on the "CBS Evening News" for 26 February 1986 described Siberia in a special series called "Behind Party Lines": "It will take more than a new five-year plan and grandiose statistics to change a Russia where you can still see women washing clothes in a frozen stream with the temperature 10 degrees below zero."

The Reagan-era images of the Soviets came through most clearly in motion pictures and product ads on television. These are cartoon pictures—exaggerated, unreal entertainment that no one is supposed to take seriously, or so we are assured by their packagers. In *Rocky IV* actor Sylvester Stallone, as stand-in for the United States, is cast as the underdog fighting against the Soviet

Union. The film is based on a clever reversal of roles. Rocky exemplifies the work ethic; he is portrayed as the backward-peasant type. The Russian fighter, Ivan Drago, is a bionic man, the product of Soviet technology (the same high-tech apparatchiks who gave the world Chernobyl!). In the 1984 motion picture *Moscow on the Hudson* we are back on familiar ground: the Russian defector faints in a U.S. supermarket upon confronting the choices of coffee available to him. But there is a 1970s sensibility, too: the hero's adopted Harlem family is like his Moscow family. In the 1980s action film *Red Dawn*, the narrative is pure Reaganite: communists invade an America that is woefully unprepared, despite all efforts at military buildup. In the staggeringly popular *Rambo* ($32 million in ticket sales in the first six days), the Stallone hero is tortured by a sinister Soviet adviser to the North Vietnamese. The *New York Times*'s David Shipler, who served as the *Times*'s Moscow bureau chief from 1977 to 1979, experienced a shock of recognition when he saw *Rambo*: "The actor played the Soviet officer just like Hollywood actors played Hitler SS men in the movies of the 1940s." Later, Rambo single-handedly reverses the outcome of the Vietnam War and declares that "to survive war, you have to become war," a message in tune with its times.

Probably no one over 14 believes that these cartoonish images reflect real life. But they do resonate with psychic reality. About this time, a half dozen TV spots for products as varied as automobile parts and hamburgers reflected the same general themes. These mid-1980s commercials ridiculed the Soviets, jabbing at their lives as devoid of choice. The unstated assumption was that, had the Russians the opportunity, they would certainly go U.S.A. all the way. The Midas Muffler commercial, for example, is all about absence of choice: camera-up on snowbound scene—the stereotypical Russian wintry picture—as identical cars move sluggishly around a traffic circle framed by red-bannered buildings. A "Russian," heavy jowled, wearing a fur hat, gratefully embraces the Midas

Man on learning that in America, unlike in his backward society, mufflers come in a variety of sizes and prices. Wendy's hamburger chain ("Have It Your Way") takes aim at lack of choice, too. A fashion show is presided over by a uniformed Russian woman, with the physique of Hulk Hogan and the face of Big Brother. While the party faithful dispiritedly applaud, another Hogan-sized harridan, wearing a formless sack, heaves her way through three showings of the same outfit, two of them differentiated only by her accessories, a flashlight for "evenink vear," a beach ball for "schvim vear."

Humor, and more, appears in other ads showing how Russians yearn for Western symbols of the good life. Soviet emigré comedian Yakov Smirnoff celebrates his discovery of such good things as "blue jeans, unopened mail, and Miller Lite." In America, he says, "You can always find a party. In Russia, party finds you." In televised spots urging citizens to play the State of Maryland lottery, Soviet cosmonauts (we know they are Russian because every word they speak ends in "ski") hope to pick the winning number and fly off with frost-free refrigerators. For Meister Brau beer, Comrade Petrinko has so thoroughiy incorporated the Western way that he embezzles funds earmarked for his superiors and uses his savings to buy a "big American automobile with tailfins," as he explains to the showroom salesman. The theme that the Russians want American goods moves into true fantasy in the RC Cola commercial depicting Russians who are willing to risk their lives for the taste of forbidden RC fruit. RC Cola is good, and it is not state-sanctioned like Pepsi.

By the late 1980s, these commercial certitudes crumbled. Mikhail Gorbachev began his attempts at *perestroika* and *glasnost*, achieved mixed results—and left American policymakers hesitant: what should the United States root for, change or collapse? Gradually, the Bush administration adopted a softer, less confrontational approach. The fall of the Berlin Wall, the democratic movements in Eastern Europe, and the general retreat of socialism within the Soviet Union produced further reevaluations of American policy. By 1990, the mixed message on Gorbachev—apparent good guy trying to achieve good works while preserving some aspects of communist power—was reflected in the ambivalence of the Bush response. *Time* magazine named Gorbachev its "Man of the Decade," while the talk show warriors of the "McLaughlin Show" sounded the conservatives' fear of a Red trick. Confused and conflicted, the image-makers of American advertising held off making *any* judgments: the Russians and Soviet themes disappeared from commercials almost overnight. In 1990, no one knew the right jokes to make any more. Journalism also turned tentative. Editors and producers would reject the notion that American media get their cues from American policymakers. But American journalists are . . . well, Americans. "We in the press are products of our culture and our society and reflect that," in the words of Lawrence Grossman, the former president of NBC News. A multiplicity of "American" policies emanate from Washington at any given time: the incumbent administration's stance, which can have a Pentagon and/or State Department and/or congressional variation; and the opposition party's stance, especially when it has a congressional majority.

The prevailing political and policy winds can carry both the press and the popular culture along. During the Nixon detente period, Nixon's administration benignly created a "Tanya" climate and the press reflected it. In the Reagan "Bear" period, the administration blew up a confrontational gale, and both the journalists and the advertising trend-spotters, attuned to atmospherics, followed in the administration's path.

At the start of the 1990s, Americans had to live with the Bush administration's uncertainty concerning Mikhail Gorbachev. When Gorbachev came to power, some American commentators expressed relief that we finally had a "modern" leader we could talk to, one whose style seemed familiar to us. Stalin, and then Khrushchev, could be patronized to a certain extent. We saw them in terms of a duality: earthy, peasantlike, emotional, but also poised on the edge of irrational outbursts and violence. Khrushchev had the "cold eyes of a peasant," David Brinkley told the country on ABC's evening news show. Then came Brezhnev, not so much a peasant as a bourgeois. "When he hears music, his eyes moisten. . . . But he has an explosive temperament, too," the *Chicago Tribune* reported in 1972. He likes physical contact, embraces, kisses, the paper said: "He wants to be loved. A typical Russian? Yes, but more than that." He likes cars, "nattily tailored suits," dancing, "toward women he is gallant." Next came the gerontocracy of Andropov and Chernenko, "impassive, often barely mobile men who seemed incapable of making the simplest announcement without a script, of taking a single step without guidance" as the *New York Times* reported on the eve of their Geneva summit meetings. Then came Gorbachev. He was something else: relatively young, relatively adroit at handling public relations, relatively open—he actually went on television to talk about Chernobyl. He was "the new Soviet man." But when he played the old Soviet power themes, relief turned to suspicion. The Bush administration was unsure how to handle him, and its uncertainty was passed on in the Washington press coverage.

Journalists complained that Gorbachev controlled the flow of information and presided over a closed society; when he used the modern skills of public relations, we complained that it was just more propaganda. At first eager to deal with someone "more like us," we backed off as we recognized certain connections between the Soviets and us. Yet as we recognize similarities, the stereotypes begin to come apart. Cartoonish thinking and ridicule had created a distance, giving a comfortable but perhaps illusory sense that the Red Threat had lessened. Currently, no one can take the measure of the new distance between the United States and the USSR. Leaders, East and West, who do not make use of the tools of propaganda are to a certain extent derelict in their duty to the modern state. But there are limits to news management. The Soviets once manipulated images with relentless energy. Their versions of U.S. society presented more caricatures than *Rocky* and *Rambo* back to back. The narrative did not work, and they have all but given up such efforts. Instead, there are the beginnings of sustained media analysis and policy criticism in the Soviet Union—and the party may be less and less able to find you if you are critical, to turn around the Yaakov Smirnoff joke. On our side, too, change and confusion have stirred new thinking; efforts are being made to get at the assumptions that underpin our media images. The old habit of tailoring fresh information to fit into the limited frame of historic clichés has become harder and harder to sustain. The freedom the American media have means we are free to adjust old images in light of new information. Perhaps the Soviets will find this Western habit worth emulating.

Mistaken Identities:
The United States and Japan

16

Since the United States occupied Japan in 1945, the two countries have been inseparable politically—the best of allies—as well as major economic partners. Now the friendly partnership is threatening to turn sour, the future going back to the past. During the war years of the 1940s, propaganda posters urged Americans to "Slap the Jap," a cartoon figure with buckteeth, Coke-bottle eyeglasses, and—in some particularly nasty versions—a bestial visage. Today the negative attitude is comparable although the imagery is more subtle: "Japan bashing" goes on, but usually in the name of "fairness" in American-Japanese trade and economic issues. Our research group started out in 1987 to study how these trade issues were being covered by U.S. news outlets. We quickly saw how media advertising, Hollywood films, television comedies, mass market books, political cartoons, and other elements of American popular culture were continuously reinforcing certain deeply held negative mental images of the Japanese.

By now, everyone knows that the United States, long the wealthiest nation in the world, has become the biggest debtor nation, while poor, defeated Japan has grown to become "Japan Inc."—and America's biggest creditor. It is a role reversal bound to have political and psychological effects, the more so when tied to memories of a brutal war. No other country quite occupies this role in the American psyche. An Iraqi warplane sent a missile into the hull of the U.S. Navy frigate *Stark* and killed 37 American sailors, but the story soon passed. Iraq continued to draw a blank in most Americans' emotional memory screens, until the Persian Gulf crisis that began in August 1990. Even then, images of the Iraqis as a people remained vague and undefined; mainly, their leader, Saddam Hussein, was demonized.

Before Japan Inc., the dominant picture of Japan in the American mind was linked to memories of World War II. Thus, anchor Tom Brokaw, reporting an economics story on the "NBC Nightly News," began by saying, "Forty years after the end of one war between them, the U. S. and Japan are trying to avoid another war, this time, a trade war." Given a steady media barrage along these lines, it is not surprising that the war that ended more than 45 years ago is still a mental reference point for many Americans. In a 1985 poll conducted jointly by the *New York Times*, CBS News, and the Tokyo Broadcasting System, Americans were asked what came to mind when Japan was mentioned. One in every five respondents named "war-related events." On the other side of the Pacific, only 7 percent of the Japanese questioned in the poll named "war-related events" when asked what first came to mind when they thought about the United States. But more recent polls of Japanese attitudes indicate that trade tensions are beginning to have their effects: more and more Japanese are reporting "unfriendly" feelings toward the United States.

U.S. images of Japan and the Japanese are, overall, negative. Too often, U.S. pop culture evokes pictures of Japanese "conformity" and "clannishness." In a United Parcel Service television advertisement, a UPS representative is shown taking twelve "Japanese businessmen" on tour. Each man is in similar dress and of similar height; they walk single file through the commercial; the men nod to each other at each sight they see; and they finally go up into the door of a brown UPS delivery van, and out the other side, while the voice-over says, "UPS. The most rewarding package tour." The commercial derives its "humor" from an assumption that we all "know" to be true: the Japanese behave as an antlike collective, protectively traveling with their own kind. Of course, Americans travel in groups, too; many people feel more comfortable that way. When the conformist image is applied to people who are already conceived of as different—inscrutable—the picture comes out negative: the Japanese are seen as either comical or threatening.

The same stereotypes can be found in late 1980s motion pictures involving Japanese characters. *Blind Date*, an otherwise forgettable vehicle for the actor Bruce Willis, presents a stiff Japanese businessman and his submissive wife, who is dressed in a geisha costume complete with lacquered wig and white face powder. Similar anachronisms appear on American television. A recent rerun of the situation comedy "Gung Ho" featured two references to ritual suicide, one to samurai warriors, one to sumo wrestling, and one to miniaturization—all within a half-hour show. Occasional favorable impressions do come through: a *U.S. News and World Report* cover story in the summer of 1987 depicted the industrious Japanese as always a step in front: "even their clocks . . . are ahead of ours." But positive or negative, these images short-circuit reasonable thinking. They reinforce pictures in our minds that often are crude to begin with.

One picture that counts in U.S.–Japanese relations is the depiction of the two countries' trade; on average, one-third of America's annual $150 billion trade deficit in the late 1980s was with Japan. The term "Japan Inc." is intended to convey the image of a country run like an efficient corporation, with business as its sole reason for existence and political ministries functioning as a board of directors. Japan Inc.'s products sold so well worldwide that many Americans believed it was necessary to learn about how business is conducted and managed in Japan in order to compete.

Books such as *Theory Z* and *Shadows of the Rising Sun* attempted to explain what had gone wrong with American business, and what is right in Japan. David Halberstam in *The Reckoning* contrasted Ford Motor and Nissan Auto and their corporate structures and leadership. Halberstam portrayed Japan's profit-oriented bureaucracy and Japanese citizens as cogs in the wheels of industry. To Americans, this system seems like a social nightmare, a denial of the spirit of individual enterprise. It also results in other nightmares, especially the specter of American jobs lost to more competitive imports and of whole towns idled as a result. It makes Americans wonder, as one worker did on a CBS News special report, "Just who did win in 1945, anyway?"

Yet modern Japan itself is a "product" made in America—or, more precisely, one that emulates America to a great extent. Immediately after World War II, the United States assumed a teacher-student relationship with its defeated enemy, much to initial Japanese consternation. The United States gave Japan a constitution and a new school system, and sent in business teams to teach corporate management and quality control. The pragmatic Japanese absorbed all these lessons. They set about rebuilding their country, adopting the best of the technology and marketing systems that the United States had to offer. Popular culture symbols do not reflect this reality. Typically, the images not only present caricatures of Japan and the Japanese, but outdated ones at that. The images reflect only a partially accurate picture, but one that is too often taken for the whole truth.

A skeptic might wonder what effect a 30-second spot, a television sitcom, a motion picture, or a network news broadcast might have on perceptions. One answer is that, eventually, skewed particulars add up to a misleading whole. Stereotypes should be recognized wherever they appear, whether in hard-news accounts or all-fluff commercials, so that we can discount the superficial and maintain some sense of balance.

Another element in Americans' stereotyped attitudes about Japan is cultural and racial. To a certain extent, Americans live in a mythic past; although the U.S. is a multiracial society, much of the American dream—for example, the ideals of rugged individualism and the winning of the West—is usually rendered in an all-white hue. As it happened, once upon a time in the West, Asians were invited to this country when their labor was needed— to build the railroads, for example. Efforts to exclude them came later. Perceptions of Japanese "inferiority" or "weakness" occur in terms of American cultural baggage. This soon becomes apparent. If West Germans dumped chips on the market or sold computers to the Soviets, would national resentment be as strong? No one hears many expressions of anti-Norwegian sentiment in the aftermath of a Norwegian company's sales of secret submarine technology to the Soviet Union. Nothing on television or in print currently reflects the blatant racism reminiscent of World War II–vintage posters; but the trade imbalance that strains U.S.–Japanese friendship has also revived American jingoism and calls for protectionism. Americans would do better to take pride in their own good sportsmanship; America has not flooded any markets with its underpriced goods, as Japan has, in both the United States and Europe. It would be healthier to remember, and take pride in, American "fairness," rather than putting down Japan and the Japanese in order to boost American feelings of worth.

The media could begin the process by rethinking the too-easy stereotypes of television comedies and 30-second advertising spots; these images are false and ultimately self-destructive. We could all profit by reevaluating old cultural notions. The inscrutable East belongs to the past. The Japanese are not ciphers; they can be understood by anyone who makes the effort. As a starting point we might remember that Japan is a capitalist nation much like the United States. The two countries share a belief in the work ethic, in progress, and in social mobility. Lately, the students have beaten the teachers at their own entrepreneurial game. That is the real image, in print and on television, that requires considerable adjustment for Americans. The Japanese are not ten-foot-tall sumo wrestlers; neither are they sneaky little schemers. Japan is a modern industrialized nation and a trading partner of America. In short, an equal. As Americans, press and public alike, begin to shed the errors of stereotypes, they will be able to see the game and the players more clearly.

In 1853, Matthew Perry of the U.S. Navy sailed into what is now Tokyo Bay, ended Japan's seclusion, and opened the island kingdom to the West. Now, American media have arrived to open the eyes of U.S. viewers to present-day Japan. The encounter may signal a shift from the mutual fears and suspicions that have been threatening to isolate Japan and the United States from each other. Specifically, television arrived in force for the funeral of Emperor Hirohito, who had occupied the throne for 62 years; on that occasion, in February 1989, the cameras closed in on Japan and the Japanese. With the funeral and the ascension of the new emperor Akihito as a pretext for attention, television offered its audiences a crash course on the "new," the "industrious," the "changing" Japan.

Many of the lessons had been taught before in newspapers and in news features and documentaries scattered around the television dial. What made this second opening of Japan so remarkable was the quality of the coverage. Politics initially opened the door. In Washington, earlier in February, George Bush had said to his guest, Japanese prime minister Noboru Takeshita, "We need one another." Bush then demonstrated the importance of Japan to the United States by making his trip to Tokyo for the February 24 funeral. The attention paid by the networks validated the occasion. It was not just a case of the press following the president. Bush also went to Beijing and Seoul, but only CBS broadcast from there: while China and South Korea were important, they were not contenders for No. 1.

Once in Japan, the networks showed what extra time and resources can accomplish. There were reports from Buddhist temples, the Japanese stock exchange, a traditional teahouse, subway cars, offices, wedding parties, classrooms, homes, restaurants, bars, hotels, and arcades. No subject was ignored: work, school, home, religion, leisure, arts, shopping, entertainment, and especially women—in the workplace, in the home, in transition—all received attention. Sometimes the crowded living conditions that the Japanese endure were inadvertently mirrored in the reports. One night Dan Rather and Peter Jennings were both recorded broadcasting as each walked on the Ginza, Tokyo's main shopping street. Half expectantly, we waited for each man to turn around on the street and encounter the other. The anchors did not collide, though some of the Americans' observations did: single Japanese women over 25, we were reminded several times during the week, are known as "Christmas cakes" because no one wants a wife after the 25th.

The best journalism came out of broadly defined themes, when reporters substituted information for stereotypes. On CNN, for example, reporters dealt seriously with the second-class status of Japanese women. "In Japan it's a man's world," Don Miller said. "For centuries man has been the master. . . . It's changing, but slowly. . . . In 1986 a new law was passed legislating equality in hiring and promotions . . . but [women] still earn half what men do." NBC, too, went beyond the cliché of "changing Japan" when correspondent George Lewis reported that Japanese youth are less work-oriented than their parents, no longer believe in lifelong loyalty to one company, and want a less regimented society. Similarly, Peter Jennings introduced an overview of the Japanese economic success. Newsreel footage of circa-1945 bombed cities illustrated his theme: "rubble to renaissance—at breathtaking speed." America was given some credit for the Japanese miracle; the United States "was instrumental in setting the Japanese back on the road to industrial success." The Japanese "copied, redesigned, improved on" U.S. products and ideas.

This last point proved critical. U.S. television responds to U.S. politics and society. When the president treats Japan as important, the news shows do the same. When ordinary Americans worry about foreign takeovers, the camera zooms in on them. The first angry voice heard on the CBS special report "America for Sale" came from an Alabama businesswoman, who said, "I haven't forgotten Pearl Harbor. . . . They're just taking money and buying [the country]." Xenophobia alone does not create the specter of American jobs lost to more competitive imports; know-nothing attitudes develop in the dark, in the absence of information. The television invasion of early 1989 framed today's Japan in more realistic terms. The commitment of resources guaranteed an unprecedented level of information for U.S. viewers. When the anchors went home, coverage reverted to the occasional minute-and-a-half news story or 30-second item, typically about political or economic developments. But larger perceptions and new images will remain in American minds. Above all, the realization that modern Japan is, in part, a "product" made in America is beginning to be understood.

The Unknockables

17

Remember the first years of the Reagan administration when Nancy Reagan was a punching bag for the press? There were negative stories about her wealthy, leisured friends, such as Betsy Bloomingdale and Jerome Zipkin, and about her own expensive taste in clothes and jewelry. She was portrayed as having an imperious social image ("Don't cry for me, Santa Barbara"). But within the space of a year, her relations with the press became more than cordial: she became a crowd pleaser, and she routinely was named to the lists of the most admired women in America for most of the late 1980s.

This image transformation was not produced by tossing a penny down the wishing well. Chance and circumstance played a part. The assassination attempt on her husband in 1985 created a reservoir of sympathy for her and her family; the economy recovered from recession and got people smiling and thinking benignly about the state of the nation. Beyond that, she was helped by what one White House aide called "the concerted operations of some very high-powered P.R. people." Sheila Tate, Mrs. Reagan's press secretary, and Michael Deaver, then resident secretary of symbolism in the White House, rearranged the props. Mrs. Reagan, as they say in the East Wing, got her own "project": drug abuse. The ladies' luncheons were canceled. The new photo opportunities included inner-city tykes and adolescent drug fighters. Nancy Reagan became an icon of grace and competence. She was unknockable—until she left the White House.

It is fascinating to track the intricate process by which reputations rise and fall, or, in a transcendent moment, become enshrined in the national consciousness, like the presidents whose faces adorn Mount Rushmore. How and why certain men and women become Rushmorean figures, or, conversely, see their images crumble, says a great deal about shifting tastes, the workings of the press, and the collective psyche. There is no single route to—or from—unknockability. As the remaking of Nancy Reagan suggests, many variables are at work. Good public relations requires good material (okay, at least some modest assets) to promote. Mrs. Reagan was never quite the featherweight she originally appeared to be. Unknockable status goes beyond mere celebrity: public icons most often have a record of achievement, they resonate in sympathy with deep national moods, and they fulfill the mercurial needs of the media. Above all, they make people feel good about any number of things: age, gender, work, but especially themselves. Not all of that can be done with mirrors and blue smoke. George Bush performed rather poorly as president on camera. Yet his approval ratings soared in his first two years in office. He was tall, fit, and not too mean—the way Americans like to see themselves.

Unassailable reputations can be linked to sweeping events: Katharine Graham and the *Washington Post*'s pursuit of Watergate, Felix Rohatyn and the fiscal rescue of New York City. Tragic myths can help: Jacqueline Kennedy Onassis remains, even today, the widow of Camelot. Walter Cronkite achieved unknockability by presiding at great public dramas: wars, assassinations, moon landings. Sometimes a single gesture, properly played, can repair a flawed resume. Norman Mailer, novelist, brawler, and Jack Abbott's amicus curiae, became a statesman of literature in the *New York Times* by raising funds for the PEN congress. Americans love comebacks, fighters, Cinderella figures, and teams: witness the public response to the first *Rocky* movie, and the early Stallone, the 1969 Mets, the 1980 U.S. Olympics hockey squad. Katharine Graham went from reticent housewife to the most powerful woman executive in America, a real-life transformation that mirrored an emerging national consensus: society needed a female CEO who had a tough but feminine image. Barbara Bush achieved iconographic status when the same consensus agreed on the value of white-haired grandmothers of good breeding. Occasionally, even people of achievement can get an extra boost from adversity. Passed over in the official balloting for an Academy Award, Steven Spielberg nonetheless won the public's vote. Longevity is a key to unknockable status. When recollection nods, an honor often wakes the public up. Robert Penn Warren's designation as the first U.S. poet laureate created a new beginning for the 80-year-old author (he died, presumably in repose, shortly afterward). Though people are usually too polite to say so, physical illness, mental anguish, and trouble with children all help create unknockables: think of Joseph Heller, Betty Ford, and Carol Burnett. Out of a sense of fairness and balance, the press and public may decide that someone has "suffered enough." The best rehabilitation of reputation takes place quietly, holistically, and well offstage—perhaps in Saddle River, New Jersey, the Elba of Richard Nixon's long penance and the base for his recent return to a degree of public favor. But durability can be risky. Ralph Nader became sanctified early, in part because General Motors made him an underdog by hiring private detectives to dig up some dirt on him. Nader still stands tall because he remains a credible symbol of personal recitude. But Gloria Steinem has not fared so well. A major heroine of the women's movement and a founder of *Ms.* magazine, Steinem sounded to some of her followers like just another upscale-advertising sales director when she defended the sappy perfume ads (for Obsession) when they appeared in her monthly.

Although the making and unmaking of a reputation follow no set rules, certain patterns exist. After studying the products of such organizations as CBS, NBC, *Newsweek*, and *Time*, sociologist Herbert J. Gans concluded that "hidden values" were reflected in the news. These "preference statements about nation and society" help the media gatekeepers select, from all the *events* of the day, those items, ideas, and personalities that will become *news*. The hidden values are enduring: the nation, the democratic system, responsible capitalism, pastoralism, individualism, and moderation. Bigness is bad, extremists are dangerous; craftsmanship is to be prized, architecture should have "a human scale." The list is almost intuitive; a night of news watching confirms the common sense of it all. Bush orders a war against Saddam Hussein and the president's ratings go up; the head of Johnson & Johnson, the makers of Tylenol, is lauded for doing the right thing, putting the commonwealth before profit when some Tylenol containers were found tampered; Dan Rather goes to the heartland to mourn the passing of the family farm.

Many values are not so hidden. Mrs. Kennedy became Mrs. Onassis and kept her money, looks, and dramatic history—the stuff of stardom. But, unlike a star, she cultivated a low profile: she avoided interviews, took a real job, and raised her kids—just like (sort of) other Americans. Her wholesome self-effacement also effaced a lingering image of greed in the Aegean. Highly visible success often produces more success, and inflates status. Rupert Murdoch breezed into New York City in 1977 and proved instantly knockable for his gamy, Fleet Street brand of journalism and brash capitalistic style. Today, the Establishment has embraced him, extending him credit for his sprawling communications empire and applauding his stewardship of the London *Times*, England's (formerly) untouchable journalistic institution.

Excess can also breed success and, handled right, put a person beyond the reach of normal criticism. Ed Koch and George Steinbrenner conducted their lives fortissimo. Knocked, they knocked back—hard. Then one day they rose, like hot-air balloons, larger than life and free of the pull of mundane judgments. Donald Trump has also gone off the scale, if only because of his sustained grandiosity: Trump Tower, Trump Plaza, Trump Shuttle, Trump at Mar-a-Lago in Palm Beach, Trump in Aspen, and Trump in *three* Atlantic City casinos. The sheer gall of his plans stonewalled the doubters—until the bankers began calling in the chits. Then, Trump was dumped on in news accounts, in keeping with the modern media's unseemly rule: kick 'em when they're down.

More conventional power can be an attractive ingredient of unknockability. While he was still in Boston, Mortimer Zuckerman was just a local real-estate developer who happened to own the *Atlantic* and was known primarily for some sticky legal squabbles; now, as proprietor of *U.S. News & World Report*, he serves on presidential commissions, writes editorials on global affairs—and has even managed to outbid Trump, landing the deal to develop the Columbus Circle site of the old Coliseum in midtown New York. Power assumes an especially irreproachable aura when it is given away. Laurence Tisch would seem to have enough on his hands with CBS, yet he can be found a couple of mornings a week at NYU, where he is active as chairman of the board of trustees. "Tisch is a rich man who gives his time and experience," says Alan Altschuler, the former dean of NYU's Graduate School of Public Administration. "That's as good as giving money." Certain positions can be vehicles for unknockability: where you sit is often where you stand. The office of the presidency ennobles the occupant until his own actions besmirch his reputations. But a few presidents, Ronald Reagan, for one, levitate magically above the facts. "On any given issue," says political consultant David Garth, "polls showed the public disagreed with Reagan. But overall, people loved him."

If the job sometimes makes the unknockable man, the man can sometimes make the unknockable job. Henry Kissinger fashioned his position as the president's national security adviser into a platform for his own stardom. When Robert C. McFarlane took over the post, in 1983, he was known as a dutiful civil servant, a former Marine Corps lieutenant colonel—"Bud" to his friends. When McFarlane left for the private sector, he signed up with the Walker Agency to lecture, at an estimated $20,000 an appearance; three universities jockeyed for his presence. That prompted the Washington media, as Michael Kinsley pointed out in the *New Republic*, to wonder why "a man of McFarlane's stature was being replaced by a person no one had ever heard of." The unheard-of-man was Admiral John Poindexter, another dutiful public servant, someone very much like Bud McFarlane before he got the national security job. The man can sometimes unmake the reputation, as well; McFarlane and Poindexter later did themselves in during the Iran-Contra scandal.

Even modest positions can be useful. "What was the New York Public Library but a pair of stone lions? And look at Vartan Gregorian now," says public relations man Howard Rubenstein, referring to the library's then-president, an energetic Manhattan unknockable of the mid-1980s. Gregorian succeeded so well at fund-raising that he made the once shabby place a sanctum of chic. Naturally, he had the assistance of such sainted patrons as Brooke Astor and Andrew Heiskell. Their most successful promotion was— what else?—the library's annual literary-lion awards. In 1989, the charming and able Gregorian ascended to his own lionhood, becoming president of Brown University.

Counterpositioning—going against trends—can also be a path to honor. If the football player William "The Refrigerator" Perry did not exist, it would be necessary to invent him. It was time for a different face on the sports pages, and The Refrigerator came forward, an embodiment of public desires and publicity savvy. Pro football's offenses and defenses had become predictable, and the advertisers' messages were going unwatched. Worse still, the game had a drug problem. Then Perry came along—overweight, but wholesomely so. At the same time, the *thin* wholesome people of the world—joggers, aerobic instructors, health nuts, all of whom had enjoyed a decade of status—were becoming boring (although Workout Jane did replace Hanoi Jane). The Refrigerator met everyone's needs.

Nobody is surprised anymore to learn that heroes have handlers. The telegossip Rona Barrett may have gone too far on the "Donahue" show, when she indignantly announced that "95 percent of what you read and see in the news is the result of press agents' handouts." (Barrett, not so incidentally, did a major job of reinventing herself in the public mind, so she is something of an authority.) But most clear-eyed journalists acknowledge that deadline pressures, the "objective" conventions of the craft, and their own loose work habits often lead to the regurgitation of press releases. Thus, by dint of sheer repetition, certain names assume a ring of authority. Some "authorities" may not need the press releases if they can make journalists' lives easier on the phone or on camera. Rae Goodell of MIT discovered the "visible scientists": people like Carl Sagan and others who pop up regularly as sources for quotes and as television commentators. They know how to make issue-oriented, controversial, articulate, colorful, credible—and short—statements. Masters of the one-liner and the fifteen-second sound bite, they are sought for their special expertise—which often consists of being expert at sounding expert. Once such a resourceful expert makes it to the Rolodexes of news organizations, the "Nightline" interviews follow. These usual suspects are given an emblematic identity, a quick title suggesting unknockable status. An analyst who appeared on the "CBS Evening News" after the battle between American and Libyan forces in the Gulf of Sidra was identified with a caption that said "Naval Expert." Television looks for the union label. Because few people had actually read anything the new poet laureate had written in recent years, the citizenry had to be reassured that Robert Penn Warren was a "Pulitzer Prize–winning author."

The expert unknockable works hard, often doing the reporter's job. "Felix Rohatyn and people like him can make you look good," says an editor with extensive personal experience. "He can give you a nugget of information or an insight and let you make it your own in the story." The media, in turn, keep the Rohatyns of the world looking good. In the 1960s, Rohatyn's work on behalf of ITT earned him the emblematic I.D. of "Felix the Fixer," though the title did not show up in many stories. Rohatyn kept burnishing his image by writing essays for the *New York Review of Books*. A few years ago, the *New Republic* took the essays apart, pointing out how far off Rohatyn had been on a number of issues. The piece had little effect on Rohatyn's media status. He was still "The Man Who Saved New York," and he still contributes to the *Review*. *Time*, in a cover story on corporate mergers, also showed its admiration for Rohatyn, running a full-page interview with him. The article began by implicitly acknowledging a certain editorial dilemma. As a senior partner at Lazard Freres, Rohatyn had engineered hundreds of mergers and acquisitions, yet *Time* was ostensibly *viewing with concern* the outbreak of takeoverism. *Time*'s deft solution: "Though he can claim credit for inventing many of the tools of modern corporate mergers, Rohatyn . . . these days is like the sorcerer whose apprentices have run amuck. . . . Said he, 'Today things are getting badly out of hand.'" The rest of the article faithfully recorded the words of the master.

There are other wizards with the power to wave their wands and turn journalists into their apprentices. When a critic writing in the *New York Times Book Review* delivered a mild rebuke to William F. Buckley, Jr., for saying that he sometimes turns out a column in 20 minutes, the aggrieved Buckley was provided with a full page in the *Book Review* for a rebuttal; less favored recipients of sour notices must be content with grinding their teeth.

As dinner-table talk, the issue of who is unknockable or knockable makes animated conversation. Analyzed more closely, it reinforces some fears about the media. Their sometime role as handmaiden to experts, sorcerers, and other unknockables may account for polls showing journalism to be among the less admired occupations, ranking with such knockable ones as psychology and sales. For some students of popular culture, the fascination with status and celebrity jeopardizes the national future. The provocative title of Neil Postman's book, *Amusing Ourselves to Death: Public Discourse in the Age of Show Business*, suggests where the author thinks America is headed. Postman begins by flashing back to an earlier, ideal America where people read books, followed arguments, thought logically, and participated in public affairs. This America, he argues, has been supplanted by our present television culture, which subsists on celebrities, emotions, and discourse-as-entertainment. The 1970s argument about whether television shapes culture or merely reflects it, Postman declares, has been settled: television has *become* culture. It follows that the TV culture and such look-alike print ancillaries as *People* magazine have produced a new breed of public figure. In a print culture, people were known and honored for ideas expressed in writing, not for their camera-readiness. Postman claims that the first 15 presidents of the United States would not have been recognized had they passed the average citizen on the street, but their ideas were familiar. Think of recent presidents, says Postman, "and what will come to your mind is an image . . . most likely a face on a television screen. . . . Of words, almost nothing will come to mind." Reagan was the great television communicator. Jesse Jackson may have won as many white, young adult supporters by appearing on "Saturday Night Live" as he did campaigning in 1984 or 1988.

But America was never the intellectual Arcadia of Postman's reconstruction. Current reports about the death of discourse are exaggerated; people of genuine achievement are still honored.

Analyses of the contents of magazines and newspaper columns over the last half-century show two opposing trends in who is being profiled and itemed. First, there has been a shift from captains of industry and inventors to entertainers and personalities, a shift from Alfred P. Sloan to Cher. More recently, there has been a resurgence of achievers. For every George Burns honored because he was still able to appear on television, there was a Lee Iacocca. The television-as-culture argument distorts the picture. Behind the screen, as Herbert Gans shows, bedrock values still exist, independent of entertainment. Lee Iacocca may be *known* through television, or, more precisely, his television spots may have promoted the idea that he "saved" Chrysler. But Iacocca's reputation rests on basic feelings, as myths must. Iacocca is the guy who was pushed by his boss, Henry Ford, and who pushed back.

Iacocca's stature gives him a shield against critics. When conflict-of-interest charges were aimed at him, they amounted to a 48-hour story. Iacocca became Teflon-coated, much like Ronald Reagan. The former president's appeal predated television, too. In a word, he had character (never mind his specific positions). "He was real," says David Garth, who advises liberal Democrats but still admired Reagan's unknockable status. Reagan and Iacocca and, says Garth, his friend and former client Ed Koch, were all gritty, authentic people. "They've all climbed mountains," Garth says. Or, to switch images, each started from way back: Reagan the ex-actor, Iacocca the dumped executive, Koch the Greenwich Village liberal. Koch, of course, eventually faltered on the impossibly steep climb when he tried for a fourth term as mayor of New York. He had overstayed his time in the public eye and had become an irritant that had to be expelled. His successor in 1989, David Dinkins, was the right man at the right time, so dignified-looking that he eased white fears and rose on the now unknockable idea that, for African Americans, "our time has come." In the Virginia governor's race that same year, Douglas Wilder offered the same image and profited from the same principle. Some commentators are now talking up Governor Wilder as a Democratic presidential candidate in 1992.

Electoral politics, however, may no longer be of major interest for the public, or even a goal for the ambitious. A number of critics have detected an evolution in what constitutes honor in America. If the admired men and women of the 1920s were work-ethic figures whose careers taught us how to make money and get ahead on the job, then the heroes of postwar America were consumption-driven, showy types who instructed us in how to spend money. Checking the indicators for the 1990s, it seems safe to conclude that the citizenry is fixed not so much on working for money or on spending it as on keeping it. A suggestion, then, for trend watchers: Look for the next unknockable hero or heroine on the bottom line.

Gotcha!: The Media as Moral Police

18

The precise time and place that journalism's new moral zealotry appeared in the 1988 presidential campaign is still a matter of debate. A good case can be made for 6 May 1987, at a crowded news conference in Hanover, New Hampshire, when Paul Taylor, a *Washington Post* reporter, asked Gary Hart, "Have you ever committed adultery?" No presidential candidate had ever been asked that question before in public, and Hart chose to avoid a direct reply. But by then *Post* reporters had already gathered enough evidence to convince their editors that they already knew the answer. The "Big A" question came to dominate the news of the Hart campaign; two days after Hanover, his candidacy was dead, and a distinct tone had been set for coverage of all the other candidates.

Once the "dynamics" of the Hart story began, says Robert Woodward, part of a Drake University research team that studied the role of the press in the 1988 campaign, "a new level of media inquiry was set for presidential politics." Other students of the media are considerably more blunt. Campaign journalism has become a "frenzy of feeding sharks," says political consultant David Sawyer. Adds Daniel Payne, who was a media adviser to the Michael Dukakis campaign, "Reporters all want to play Mike Wallace. They're trying to trap you." The traps have been sprung regularly. By late

September 1987, Senator Joseph Biden was gone from the campaign, after the *New York Times*, NBC News, and the *Des Moines Register-Tribune* all reported that he had plagiarized part of a speech made by Neil Kinnock, the British Labour party leader. Within a week, more blood was in the water. The two senior managers in the Dukakis campaign—the aides who had passed on videotape evidence of Biden's plagiarism and then had tried to deny their complicity—were gone. Then, in the space of ten days, the two reverends running for president, Marion G. "Pat" Robertson on the Republican side, and Jesse Jackson on the Democratic side, were under fire. On 6 October the *Wall Street Journal* reported that Robertson had fiddled with his vital biographical statistics to conceal the fact that his wife was pregnant when they married, in 1954. Even as Robertson was denouncing the press for "prying," the *Atlanta Journal-Constitution* reported that Jackson's wife was pregnant when they married, in 1962. And after sex came money: the *New York Times* disclosed that Jackson had committed himself to appear in print and broadcast ads for a national chain of business schools.

All this media frenzy, from Gary Hart on, centered on what became known as "the character issue," the all-purpose morality story of Campaign 1988. That is, if (supply name of candidate) can not handle (supply category of transgression), then how can voters trust him in the White House when dealing with (supply serious problem: nuclear weapons, the deficit, or whatever)? The case for pursuit of "character" by the press was made most forcefully by Max Frankel, executive editor of the *New York Times*, when he defended his paper's decision to explore the private conduct of candidates. The candidates themselves have "paraded their wives and families and fidelity to family values before the public by way of claiming certain character and personality traits," Frankel observed in a memo to the *Times* staff in the summer of 1987. "Where these claims turn fraudulent, they are as noteworthy as any other serious misrepresentation to the electorate." But Michael Kinsley, editor of the *New Republic*, provided a different perspective on the often mindless way the media chase after the character story; he concocted a news item, datelined Des Moines, describing how a "tearful" Senator Paul Simon had to withdraw from the 1988 race because several of his aides had failed to wash their hands before a lemonade social at a local schoolhouse. According to Kinsley, Simon might have been able to ride out the revelations, except that the *Times* was about to publish a story saying that the staffers had not brushed their teeth afterward or sent thank-you notes, either.

First Amendment purists have no problems with a press committed to full and absolute disclosure. If Hart womanized or Biden plagiarized, then the media must "put it in the paper." Journalists are only doing their jobs by reporting all the facts; their readers and viewers deserve no less. If journalists were to withhold information, even of the smarmiest sort, that would be censorship. Furthermore, press concern about character is not all that new. George McGovern had to drop Tom Eagleton as his vice-presidential running mate after the newspapers reported that Eagleton had failed to disclose that he had been hospitalized for "mental exhaustion" and had twice received electric-shock treatments—and this was in 1972, before the media's part in the Watergate scandal changed news reporting and made investigative journalism fashionable once again. In 1988, however, the character issue was pursued with an intensity unmatched in previous campaigns. Reporters at times appeared to cast themselves in the twin roles of police and judge, first aggressively catching the criminal-candidates and then adamantly enforcing new law. Sometimes, the sentence was mild enough: Dukakis escaping with only a reprimand for "not acting decisively enough" because he did not fire his aides at once. The club directors admonishing a member to wear tie and jacket in the dining room. Other times, the reporting moved along with barely concealed glee, as when the Reverend Robertson, the evangelical crusader devoted to "family values," and the Reverend Jackson, the apostle of Black Pride, appeared to fulfill stereotypical roles as, respectively, hypocrite and stud. In some extreme cases, the campaign journalists behaved like revolutionary block committees: Hart y Biden, a paredon!

Any number of other people and principles were also pushed to the wall. When news organizations decide to go all-out in pursuit of a certain story line, they are not only making a value-free "hard news" call but also a more specific moral decision. Allocations of editorial resources such as reporters' time, news-column space, and daily follow-up flow out of some prior group judgment. Everette Dennis, of the Gannett Center for Media Studies at Columbia University, suggests that the media have become "moral teachers," monitoring and enforcing "American values." Because various polls show that the public ranks "moral integrity" as the prime value sought in leaders, Dennis says, "I see nothing wrong with the press's concern if that's what is on the public's mind." Well, maybe. Marital fidelity is certainly an "American value," and many people actually believe that adultery should be punished. But is there really wide ethical agreement on the crimes involved and the punishments required in creative resume writing or slippery staff work? Even granting for the sake of argument that upon announcing, the candidate surrenders his or her rights—to personal privacy, to practicing a little intellectual dishonesty—the voters are still entitled to their rights. An ABC News–*Washington Post* poll published just before Biden's withdrawal disclosed that a majority of those questioned believed Biden should have continued his campaign. Other public opinion polls suggested that many voters thought Hart should have stayed on. William Schneider, an analyst and polling specialist, noted in the *National Journal* that these results "do not mean that people were not bothered by what Hart and Biden did or that they would have voted for them. What they reveal is widespread displeasure over the fact that the press seemed to force these candidates out of the race without consulting the voters."

Again, complaints about an assertive press in the political process are hardly new. Henry Kissinger, in his 1982 book *Years of Upheaval*, worried about a political journalism that tried to be both "neutral conduit and tribunal . . . spectator and participant." In 1988 the concern was not so much with the initial attacks as with the ferocity of the follow-up stories: the piling-on has become newsworthy itself. "The press used to beat up on us for 'manipulating the process,' " says political consultant Sawyer. "The stories may be legitimate, but the frenzy of moral hysteria is not."

The reasons the media seemed to be playing character cop in the 1988 campaign relate both to the special circumstances of contemporary presidential politics and to some long-term changes in political journalism. With no incumbent running for president for the first time since 1972, the 1988 race attracted a dozen-odd candidates. They were more or less of equal stature: all somehow seemed not tall enough. George Bush, the candidate with the best resume, had had to fight his "wimp" image. When Biden was still a candidate, the Democrats were called "The Seven Dwarfs" in the newspapers; after Biden's departure, Dukakis pushed the term "the six pack" as a macho improvement.

Both Democratic and Republican teams were condemned for being not only short but slow as well. The openness of the race forced each candidate to make an early start on his campaign, as did the current campaign-finance laws and the peculiarities of the caucus and primary system. Campaign reporters thus had the candidates to kick around for a year and a half. Also, apart from Robertson with his evangelicals and Jackson with his black supporters, the candidates did not have strong, discernible constituencies. When Biden's campaign began to come apart, there were no organized interest groups to help him stand up to the character cops. As Adam Clymer, a senior editor at the *New York Times*, told a meeting on politics and the press at the University of Illinois, "No one from the auto workers' union was saying, 'Joe Biden has been a strong friend of ours, and because we need him, we're putting these charges behind us.' " The candidates, vulnerable from the start, were easy to kick around once they were down. Equally to the point, very few issues of substance divided the two packs. The Democratic candidates grouped slightly to the left of center (with Jackson an exception) and the Republicans slightly to the right (Robertson not included). On the few occasions when one candidate or another tried to distance himself from his rivals—Albert Gore's support of the Grenada invasion, for example—relatively few people noticed. In the absence of compelling issues of public policy—or, at any rate, in the absence of the candidates' articulation of such issues—it was inevitable that news stories and analyses would home in on "character."

Unfortunately, the behavior of a succession of presidents over the last three decades helped create the character issue: John Kennedy's sexual exploits (retrospectively covered), Lyndon Johnson's deceits, and Richard Nixon's deviousness all made the case for closer scrutiny of the individual. Later, the "decent" Gerald Ford and Jimmy Carter ("I'll never lie to you") offered the chance for a more positive story line concerning character. For a time, Ronald Reagan confounded his critics, who put him down as "merely" an actor. In fact, in 1980 Reagan offered a campaign of substance, one strong on issues and high in content: he promised to cut taxes, increase defense spending, and stand up to the Soviets. By 1984, though, Reagan was running as the personable leader-host of the nation-show. The Reagan campaign used television spots that promised, "It's morning again in America." His genial personality made us feel good. "Reagan gave us a new mood in politics," says Dan Payne. "He created a soft presidency, like soft-rock radio." For a time, the deeper currents of "character" were supplanted by concerns for more surface qualities. That, at any rate, was the "real" Reagan: the actor and GE representative whose time in the presidency represented a break from his life's career. No wonder "personality" became a topic to be covered and a basis for judgment of the ability to lead.

By this time, too, there was no shortage of political analysts on call in the media. A generation ago, Theodore White could travel around Wisconsin or West Virigina with the candidate, an advance man, and a driver—all of them in one car. White not only was examining sparsely covered territory; he was a reporter in love with politics and politicans, becoming positively lyrical when he recorded the workings of the American electoral process. But between October 1987 and February 1988—almost a full year before election day—2,000 journalists dropped into Iowa for the caucuses. They came more as combative paratroopers than as lyric poets. When White was putting together his quadrennial campaign histories, he and a small band of journalists from the three commercial networks, the wire services, and three or four major newspapers carried the burden of "serious" political reporting. More remote figures, such as Walter Lippmann and James Reston, reminded members of the rules, speaking with detached objectivity and a certain agreed-upon morality.

Today, the changing ranks of the media rule-makers can be measured in a variety of ways. One is the list of the news organizations that sponsored the candidates' debates between 28 October 1987 and 6 March 1988; the list included, in addition to ABC, CBS, and NBC, the *Atlanta Journal-Constitution*, the *Boston Globe*, Cable News Network, the *Dallas Morning News*, and the *Des Moines Register-Tribune*. The competition among these new influentials has increased with their numbers. The traditional drive to be first with the story is now matched by the challenge to be bold or precedent-setting. One of the side benefits that the editors of the *Miami Herald* cherished from their surveillance of Gary Hart's Capitol Hill townhouse was the location of the big story: the reporters beat out the great *Washington Post* in its own backyard.

Certainly, the volume of political news has grown. CNN churns out news and features 24 hours a day. Headlines have to be freshened, or "retopped," hourly. Stories may take new turns after-hours, for example, in an interview on ABC's "Nightline." More does not necessarily mean better or more reflective. *USA Today* and the network news programs are models of compression. At times, the national news machine may resemble a coal-mining conveyor biting off chunks of the news and spitting them back along an endless loop. Nor is it just the old "hard facts" of the news that are now being mined. Along with increased news tonnage, there is an expanded definition of what a "news story" may be. The success of *People* magazine in the seventies offered lessons to political editors of the eighties about the attractions of personality journalism and providing the readers with the inside dope on private lives. When campaign media managers reconsider, in repose, the Hart and Biden stories, they claim that the candidates were finished off as much by the velocity of communications as by the messages of wrongdoing. The information flow, to use David Sawyer's term, developed so rapidly that the campaigns lost control of events. Gary Hart had been involved in national politics for a decade and a half, and stories about his "womanizing" had circulated among members of the press almost as long, before the *Miami Herald* and the *Washington Post* got on his case and made an insiders' story a public story. Biden's borrowings from the thoughts of others went undetected for a couple of weeks; that was why Dukakis's man John Sasso decided to speed up the process by putting together the attack videocassette.

The news of Biden developed at a horse-and-buggy pace in September 1987. The following month, Pat Robertson announced his candidacy in Brooklyn on 1 October; only five days later, the Robertsons' wedding-date story was included in a *Wall Street Journal* profile of the candidate. In the case of Jesse Jackson, the media coverage was virtually preemptive, a missile-age strike. The *Chicago*

Sun Times ran the story of the Jacksons' wedding date in the same Sunday edition that carried the account of his formal presidential announcement.

Most of all, the values of the news media have changed. The range of "permissible" subjects has broadened throughout the popular culture in the last two decades, in movies, theater, the arts, mass-market books, late-night television, and radio talk shows. The institutional culture of the news media, traditionally conservative and among the last to unbend—"We are a family newspaper," goes the familiar threnody of editors—strives now to appear as knowing as Johnny Carson or Dr. Ruth. In October 1987 Mike Wallace interviewed Jackson and his wife on CBS's "60 Minutes." Wallace played "Trapper Mike" only intermittently; Mrs. Jackson had said she would not permit any "vulgar questions." Her preemptive strike prevailed . . . for that day. However, Wallace's CBS colleague Lesley Stahl and the *Wall Street Journal* put the question about "marital fidelity" to Jackson later that same week. To each of his interrogators, Jackson invoked his personal rights, arguing that "private moral questions have no part in a campaign." Looking at the record of the campaign of 1988, he and the other candidates lost the argument, decisively.

Campaign '88: Onward and Downward

19

The end came not a moment too soon. Could anybody take one more political columnist's grandiose memo to the presidential candidates about the speech they should give, or one more mind-numbing attack of the polls commissioned by the giant combine of ABC/CBS/NBC/CNN/*New York Times/Wall Street Journal/Washington Post/USA Today*? Perhaps the media coverage of the 1988 presidential race was not as bad as it seemed at the time. Indeed, the campaign reporting was thorough and in some respects the least frivolous in memory. But the election was not about competence, whether for journalists or for Michael Dukakis. Clarity was the key to success. Yet there was—heretical idea!—too much media coverage stretched over too long a period of time: as a result, the basic 1988 campaign narrative line became obscured. The story all along was, Would there be a third Reagan administration, albeit one presided over by George Bush and whatshisname? One political commentator had it right from the start, when he wrote in the winter of 1988, after Senator Bob Dole's win in Iowa, that Bush was still the man to beat among the Republicans and that none of the Democratic aspirants could win in November, absent a national recession. The analyst was Richard Nixon, writing in the London *Times*.

There were some other unexpected stars among the campaign press corps. ABC News's team of Peter Jennings, an outsider born and raised in Canada, and David Brinkley, born in 1920, developed steadily to become the best anchor combination on television. When Brinkley began to flag on election night, whether from fatigue or boredom, reporters Jeff Greenfield and Lynn Sherr helped pick up the pace. Yet the truer measure of press performance in 1988 involved not individual efforts but media organizations as a whole. The media's achievements and shortcomings were institutional ones. Six elements of the campaign of 1988 are worth reviewing, with an eye on 1992, and beyond:

1. *Overinterpretation*   Normally in presidential primaries the electorate is indifferent and volatile: relatively few people pay attention and those that do have few firm preferences. All this makes prediction hazardous. The experts went ahead with their prognostications anyway—and gave us Bob Dole's surge, the power of the Reverend Pat Robertson's righteous army, and the prospect of the Reverend Jesse Jackson's coming time.

2. *Quayle Hunt*   The party conventions were designed to create pretty pictures for television, but they also attracted 10,000 journalists looking for news . . . and suddenly Dan Quayle flew into view. Initial media questions about the prodefense senator and his nest in the National Guard during the Vietnam years were legitimate; subsequent noisy pursuit of the story, however, worked to Quayle's advantage. After ten days of taking hits about events 20 years ago, Quayle became the beneficiary of public sympathy. The fire went out of the hunt—and Quayle's more recent mediocre record in the Senate got a press pass. He entered office as he had first appeared: an enigma.

3. *Out of Character*   The affair of Gary Hart and Donna Rice stirred media interest in the candidates' personal lives. The "character issue" was dutifully explored early in the campaign, yet much of the electorate was just beginning to focus in on the candidates

in September and October. These late tuners had only Polaroid snapshots of character, rather than clear fixes. But by then, the press had moved on to the big autumn story—the horse race of who was ahead in the polls.

4. *Losing Control*   Just as there were battleground states in the campaign, so too there were battleground voters, those whom the pollsters classify as "don't knows" and "undecideds." Bush reached these voters where they were: at home watching television. His political commercials were more focused and thus more memorable than the Dukakis output; they were also dirtier. Bush's $30 million television advertising campaign was money well spent. He also got his dollar's worth out of the daily media events staged for the evening news. Both campaigns had figured out quite early that the national networks would allot on average four or five minutes a night for coverage of the race. The format was fixed: one or two introductory paragraphs by the anchor; then, on videotape, the Republicans' "day" and the Democrats' "day," each with a correspondent's appearance and words to "wraparound" the pictures; finally, a "floater" correspondent, usually a senior reporter assigned to move between the two campaigns, would offer an assessment of the strategy behind each candidate's "day" and a one- or two-line prediction about how these calculations would affect the race. A simple stopwatch check showed that there would be time for only 30 or 40 seconds of each candidate's "day" and within that period perhaps 9 or 10 seconds for any one candidate's words. (Two years after the campaign, the analyst Kiku Addato at Harvard published statistics confirming my own stopwatch study; Addato reported that the candidate's sound bite in 1988 averaged 9.8 seconds.)

The candidates' need to master this preordained news format was obvious, as was the best way to use the precious seconds. Again the Bush side decisively seized the opportunity. His campaign media advisers would sharpen a line to serve as that night's sound bite (say, an attack on Dukakis for favoring "furloughs for murderers").

The advisers would also arrange a telegenic setting for the chosen words, creating a sight bite to accompany their sound bite. Because any spontaneity or unplanned campaign activity during the day might "step on the message," news conferences by candidate Bush were all but abolished. All too often, the political reporters assigned to Bush were reduced to watching his campaign like the rest of the country—on television.

5. *Process vs. Substance*   To the reporters' credit, this media story was well told. Roger Ailes and Peggy Noonan—respectively, Bush's media consultant and his chief speech writer—became household names. Their celebrity was not the result of their visibility in the campaign; it happened because the media talked constantly about Ailes's and Noonan's handiwork. He masterminded the negative commercials aimed at Dukakis; she crafted such lines as "a thousand points of light" and "a kinder, gentler" America. Ailes's work was closely monitored, and his negative advertising spots for Bush were "answered" in journalists' news analyses well before the Dukakis media campaign got itself together enough to respond to their opponent's methods. All told, the stories about Ailes, Noonan, and the techniques of the campaign seemed to be in the news more than traditional issues.

The interest in "process" at times overwhelmed interest in substance. Political writer Jon Margolis of the *Chicago Tribune* complained that "professors who profess to be experts on the efficacy of TV" were being interviewed more frequently than experts on foreign policy. Still, a number of news organizations found intelligent ways to cover substantive stories. The "MacNeil/Lehrer News Hour" on PBS and the *New York Times* both featured the candidates' basic stump speeches. *Newsweek*'s clever little chart, "The Conventional Wisdom," regularly offered readable insights concerning both process and substance.

6. *Poll Madness*   The people who conduct public opinion polls are far more sophisticated today than they were in 1948, when

Gallup stopped asking people about their choice between Harry S Truman and Thomas Dewey two weeks before election day. In theory, publication of poll results is not supposed to influence voters' subsequent behavior. Specifically, polling specialists argue against any bandwagon effect, that is, the movement of undecided voters toward the candidate consistently leading in the polls. In practice, so many elements go into the decision about who to vote for, or to stay home, that no one knows the cause-effect relationships. Dukakis seems to have *gained* votes in the final weekend before election day, at a time when all the polls were saying he was sure to be the loser. Hal Bruno, ABC News's political director, acknowledges that "more research" into polling effects is needed—the standard response. Ocean dumpers and others singled out as polluters of the land, air, or water usually call for additional environmental studies, too. Not only purists regard polling as a kind of campaign pollution; a majority of the public thought the media had given too much prominence to the polls, according to (what else?) a CBS News/*New York Times* poll. None of this will slow the rush to quantify; when a technology exists, it is used. The networks' defense is the expected one: we can not suppress the news. Of course, polls are not real news; they are media-made news. NBC, for example, mobilized 2,400 people to hand out NBC-designed questionnaires to voters leaving the NBC-designated bellwether precincts in order to replicate an NBC model of the general electorate. Without the NBC effort, there would have been no exit-poll results for NBC to report as "news."

The 1988 campaign enters the record books with a number of such ambiguous achievements: the most negative presidential advertising campaign in three decades, the most extensive use of horse-race polling ever, the most sophisticated application of exit-poll analyses. The campaign also provoked a record number of postmortems, the Dukakis wake aside. Jeff Greenfield, the able analyst at ABC News, proposed a way out of the constricted evening news format that allows for only sound bites and strategic assessments. He proposes . . . not a change in the networks' way of doing stories but a pledge by the candidates to change *their* ways. Greenfield wants them to forswear the punchy applause line in their speeches and the staged photo opportunity in favor of speeches that will state the candidates' "convictions and principles." The television sight bite used by the networks would still be brief, but the television sound would be more high-minded. Jonathan Alter of *Newsweek* puts a bit more of the burden of change where it belongs, on the journalists; he proposes a rerun policy wherein the exploratory character studies that television does at the beginning of the process would be offered again in the fall, when the less attentive voters are starting to tune in to the campaign.

Welcome as these changes may be, they represent rearrangements of the deck chairs on the *Titanic* of media campaigns. The basic structures remain in place. No one really needs a poll, or a critic, to know that the Bush campaign of 1988 has become an instant classic, a textbook case of media control. It worked; that is, the candidate it intended to benefit won. Others will now absorb the lessons of the Bush campaign, and emulate them. So, I will make a safe political prediction: if you liked the mean-spirited media campaign of 1988, you will love 1992.

The Yawn of a New Day

20

The morning after Martin Luther King Day, in January 1990, correspondents assigned to the White House arrived at their West Wing cubicles to discover that they had nothing to cover. President George Bush would be in "staff meetings," a press office advisory said. Then, around 1:00 P.M., a voice on the pressroom loudspeaker announced, "Travel pool . . . fifteen minutes." As one of the pool reporters later recalled, "We piled into a motorcade, not knowing where we were going or what we were supposed to write about." Fifteen minutes later, Bush and Jack Kemp, secretary of the Department of Housing and Urban Development, descended on a public housing project across the Potomac in Alexandria, Virginia, to show their "solidarity" with residents fighting drug-dealers in the area.

It was not much of a story—or, more accurately, it was a noteworthy event almost impossible to translate into a fleshed-out report for the evening news or the front page. "With no advance notice from the press office, we couldn't do any of the background reporting or videotape preparation needed to get a drugs-and-crime package on the air," says the pool reporter. "Kemp did all the talking, and Bush looked bored after a few minutes—he never has learned Reagan's technique of projecting deep interest for the benefit of the cameras." As a result, the Alexandria visit became a ten-second item on the "CBS Evening News," reported without pictures. The next morning, the *Washington Post* buried its six-paragraph story on the bottom of page 5 in the "Metro" section; the *New York Times* carried no story about the visit at all.

The Bush White House's casual approach to coverage was not a one-time fumble. A more elaborately planned antidrug visit to Kansas City the following week fared no better, because the White House simultaneously began an intense lobbying effort for its China policies—in effect, stepping on the president's own lines. White House press regulars are not yet demanding that they be manipulated in the grand old Reagan manner. But their faces and bylines appear on television and in print in proportion to how much news the White House makes. Consequently, a pervasive unease exists in the Washington news business; an assignment at the White House, once regarded as the best beat in town, no longer guarantees airtime and front-page play. In the past, the presidential beat was a great career step: just ask such former White House reporters as Tom Wicker, Russell Baker, Dan Rather, and Tom Brokaw. Today, few people can recite the names of the correspondents assigned to the Bush White House.

Some Washington journalists argue that the White House beat has long been overrated, that the press is kept confined and is regularly spoon-fed official news. "The golden bird cage," one correspondent calls it. Another reporter, who has been assigned to Bush since the 1988 election, says that he sometimes feels as if he is in a locker room during a football game. "I can't see anything, but I can hear the roar of the crowd, so I know something must be happening." At the Bush White House, the news rations have turned out to be skimpy as well as bland, and the roar just a murmur. Neither Bush nor his chief of staff, John Sununu, worry much about how the White House plays on the network news or in the elite newspapers. But the press corps cares, and nostalgia for the first heady days of the Reagan revolution flourishes. Back in the early eighties, Reagan's slick media manager, Michael Deaver, made sure that there was a theme of the day to feed the press newshounds and a good photo opportunity for the cameras of the networks' evening news programs. Leave it to Deaver: well in advance of the trip to boost the administration's war on drugs in Alexandria, he would have figured a way around security problems at the housing project. Deaver would have created tableaux vivants for the president, and for the press.

Granted, the extraordinary run of Eastern European news displaced a lot of presidential coverage during Bush's second year in office. On six consecutive days between 14 January and 20 January 1990 the *Washington Post*'s lead stories focused on Gorbachev and his troubles in Lithuania and Armenia. But that week, with Congress out of town and the local professional football team, the *Washington Redskins*, out of the league play-offs, Bush managed to make page 1 of the *Post* only once, and then the story was sleep inducing: a routine account of a White House diplomatic mission to Manila. More important, although often overlooked in talk about the Deaverization of the presidency, Reagan made real news for the press corps. He created headlines, battling, and later embracing, the Soviets; turning around 40 years of domestic public policy; speaking out on the conservatives' red-meat issues, such as abortion, military buildup, and "big government." Bush, by contrast, offered little more than an unmemorable sound bite when Chinese tanks rolled into Tiananmen Square or when the Berlin Wall fell and Eastern Europe's repressive regimes were overthrown. It took the Iraqi invasion of Kuwait to thrust a "decisive" Bush into the center of media attention.

By all accounts, Bush knows the government bureaucracy and is a vastly better White House manager than Reagan was. Bush understands the importance of controlling leaks, the mother's milk of Washington journalism. When Reagan was off chopping underbrush or riding on horseback with wife Nancy at the California ranch, his cabinet and advisers were conducting their own press relations by means of trial balloons and background interviews with favored reporters and commentators. "We had George Shultz versus Caspar Weinberger, moderates versus hardliners; it was a time of real policy wars," says a senior editor at the *Washington Post*. "Now, with Bush, there are no leaks, no turf wars, no fights over ideology. Just this gray, gray administration." Howell Raines, a former White House correspondent and now Washington bureau chief of the *New York Times*, is more circumspect: "Reagan's was a radical administration; Bush's is a custodial one."

Statistics also reflect the differences between an activist White House and a passive one. In his first year in office Bush got less than a third of the television news time that Reagan did in 1981, his first year as president. In the same period, however, Bush gave 33 full-scale news conferences and held scores of impromptu meetings with the press. Reagan had only 48 news conferences during his entire eight years in office. The conclusion is compelling: if Bush has been more accessible, he has also been considered a lot less newsworthy. And his cabinet is considered so gray that it has become almost invisible. According to the Center for Media and Public Affairs, a research group based in Washington, Millie, the Bush family dog, was mentioned on the evening news shows in the first year of the Bush presidency more often than the secretaries for education, agriculture, and veterans affairs—for the record, respectively, Lauro Cavazos, Clayton Yeutter, and Edward Derwinski. Of course, Millie had six puppies in March 1989; the three cabinet officers only presided over a combined budget of $104 billion.

Attention to the First Dog points to a certain lack of seriousness in Washington news judgment. But another set of numbers suggests that the amount of White House coverage, whether weighty or frivolous, bears little relationship to the president's standing with viewers and readers. During the same time that Bush was getting cut from the evening news and front pages, his approval ratings were rising in the polls. At the end of Bush's first year in office, a *New York Times*/CBS News Poll showed that three out of every four Americans approved of Bush, the highest such rating since John F. Kennedy's in 1961. The invasion of Panama helped boost Bush's ratings, as quick military "victories" often do for presidents; but Bush's approval figures were running as high as 70 percent even before Noriega was snared and shipped to the United States.

Perhaps a president does not need a lot of good media coverage to run the country—just low inflation and military successes. "The conventional wisdom," says Brit Hume, ABC's White House correspondent, "is that you had to have a commanding presence on television in this era, to deliver a great speech, to rally a nation." But Bush's speeches are at best "utilitarian," to use Hume's term. "We journalists are thinking, We're dying; how are we going to do anything with this for TV?" "And yet," he says, "Bush is doing fine without any inspiring rhetoric." And, Hume could add, without a lot of press attention, either.

Perestroika

The Incurious Eye

21

One spring day in April 1986, not long after General Electric acquired RCA, the parent company of NBC, David Letterman decided to visit the GE Building on Lexington Avenue in New York City. Wearing a varsity jacket and jeans, he took along a videotape crew from his "Late Night" show, as well as a basket of fruit. As Letterman explained to the camera, with a hint of a grin, he wanted to meet his new bosses, discuss what effects the takeover might have on programming, and drop off the fruit as a gesture of good will. Letterman never got the meeting he wanted: GE security guards ordered him away from the elevators, behaving with the naiveté about the media that came to characterize GE's stewardship of the network in the first years of the new order. Letterman's "Late Night" fans saw the episode on his program: three minutes of corporate comedy before a GE security chief put his hand over the camera and ended the fun.

David Letterman aside, the rest of NBC, and specifically its news operations, showed little professional curiosity about the new owners. Nor did ABC or CBS do much better at covering themselves. ABC's evening news program, "World News Tonight," decided that the takeover of ABC by Capital Cities Communications was worth just two short items during the week of 18 March 1985; the "CBS Evening News" devoted only two minutes and

20 seconds to the story of Laurence Tisch's assumption of control of the CBS network during the week of 7 September 1986. When ABC's and CBS's writers went out on strike in March 1987, ABC's Peter Jennings made a bare-bones note of the walkout at the end of his newscast.

The last few years have been tumultuous ones for broadcasting. The push toward deregulation in Washington, together with the casino climate on Wall Street, put many communications companies' stocks into play and culminated in a change of leadership at each of the three old-line networks. Capital Cities' acquisition of ABC, in March 1985, marked the first time since 1953 that one of the three major television networks had changed hands. The acquisition was page-1 news. Each of the three networks began its broadcast for Monday, 18 March, with the story. Anchor Peter Jennings's lead on "World News Tonight" set the tone for ABC's coverage: "We have seen the news and it is us," Jennings said, paraphrasing a famous line from the "Pogo" comic strip. Next, correspondent Lynn Sherr sketched the background of the two companies and raised the proper question of what the merger might mean to the network's news and entertainment programming. But her answer offered no more than conventional wisdom. Capital Cities chairman Thomas Murphy was heard saying that he would follow a hands-off policy with both news and entertainment. So much for a discussion of the likely impact of frugal Capital Cities on the big-spending colossus ABC, with its fabled executive styles of "layers, lawyers, and limousines." On the "CBS Evening News" Dan Rather read the headlines and then announced, "Ray Brady looks at what this may mean, from the business and broadcast executive set to what you see on your home TV set." But business correspondent Brady offered little analysis of either subject, concentrating instead on the money involved and the effects of the merger on ABC's share price on Wall Street. On the "NBC Nightly News," Tom Brokaw treated the story much the same way, sticking to the bare business facts. NBC's chief financial correspondent, Mike Jensen, had the presence to point out that although Capital Cities was a company one-fourth the size of ABC, it nevertheless earned a profit almost as large. But left up in the air was the intriguing follow-up question of what had caused ABC's apparent poor performance. Jensen closed his report with the brief observation, "ABC's programming is not likely to change, at least for now." ABC's "World News Tonight" was the only evening news program to present a follow-up story the next day. Correspondent Stephen Aug moved the story ahead: "Within the broadcast business there was some feeling the ABC/Capital Cities merger would not be an isolated case." But no network provided any background on the series of FCC rulings that had made the era of mergers possible, after 30 years of rigid status quo in broadcasting.

By early December 1985, General Electric and RCA had nearly reached an agreement on their deal. With the prospect of a second takeover to cover, television news had another good opportunity to examine its own business. Once again, they met the news—and avoided it. On 11 December, Mike Jensen on NBC noted that trading was frantic in RCA stock, which had gone up an "astonishing" 20 percent. Jensen reported, in the just-folks manner of someone talking about a neighborhood store, that GE would like to get into broadcasting in a "major way." The merger was reported late that night and confirmed the next day. On the "NBC Nightly News" for 12 December Jensen reassured viewers that GE chairman John Welch had promised that GE would not interfere with NBC entertainment or news programming. A short history of NBC followed, then the story quoted consumer advocate Ralph Nader, who was seen declaring, "This GE takeover, financed heavily by tax loophole gains, is bad for competition, further concentrates power in the corporate area, and should invite a Justice Department investigation under the antitrust laws." The bedrock issues of competition and concentration were being raised, briefly and for the only time—and just as quickly were dropped.

On ABC's "World News Tonight" the same day, Lynn Sherr explained in general terms what businesses GE and RCA were in, and then informed viewers that NBC programming would stay independent. NBC chairman Grant Tinker offered reassurance: "In this day and age, there is not managed programming and certainly not managed news." Then Sherr provided a summary: "While it [the merger] may not change what you see on television, it is certainly changing the face of corporate America." It was a dramatic ending, but no one had explained what the new face of corporate America now resembled or what features had been altered.

CBS presented the story in the most compact form, sticking closely to the facts of the deal and not touching on news or programming. A stock market analyst, James Magid, was brought in to pronounce the experts' benediction: "The people at NBC News are going to be happy. After all, they are the jewel in the crown and they're going to be kept polished." His prediction turned out to be spectacularly wrong: the NBC News staff was reduced, with 300 jobs eliminated in the first year of GE's stewardship, and more eliminated in the following year. Some jewel, some polishing.

The ascension of Laurence Tisch at CBS was a more diffuse story. CBS had been in the news throughout 1985 as it successfully fended off more or less serious takeover attempts by the conservative Fairness in Media group affiliated with Senator Jesse Helms (R–N.C.); by the cable television entrepreneur Ted Turner; and by the arbitrageur Ivan Boesky (later to serve prison time for illegal stock trading). Of the three network evening news shows, CBS gave by far the most time to its own ongoing story, but the corporate end-game got much less attention. Beginning in October 1985, the Tisch family increased its Loews Corporation holdings of CBS stock to just under 25 percent (once holdings go over the 25 percent mark, government regulations require full disclosure of purchases). Although aspects of the developing story were reported sporadically, CBS viewers were for the most part unprepared for the events that took place in September 1986. It was in print, not on CBS, that the CBS story was told. *Newsweek* magazine, for example, reported in detail CBS executive-suite clashes, managerial infighting, and a mounting rebellion in the news division. Meanwhile, all CBS offered was Dan Rather's cryptic sign off, "Courage." CBS gave its audience the impression that "something is going on, but we can't tell you what it is." Then, on 9 September, ABC's "World News Tonight" devoted four minutes and 40 seconds to a chronicle of the events leading up to the CBS board meeting to be held the next day. Reported Peter Jennings, "When CBS is in trouble, as it appears to be, not only we in the industry, but millions of people in the country want to know why." An interested viewer might reasonably ask why, then, did television have to take its cue from print to cover the story? The same week, "NBC Nightly News" focused, finally, on the people involved. Mike Jensen noted the firings of hundreds of men and women, "huge problems with the profits and ratings," and "rebellion in the news division." Jensen's words were noteworthy, because it was the first time in the coverage that television news actually let the audience in on what everyone in television newsrooms was talking about. The "CBS Evening News" ran no takeover reports before the decisive CBS board meeting. Ray Brady later recalled, "I remember gnashing my teeth, watching the ABC and NBC stories. I guess at that point we were maybe afraid of overkill."

The next day, none of the three networks could report the full story because the CBS board meeting went on for nine and a half hours and was not yet over when the evening news programs went on the air. On NBC, Brokaw noted the all-day meeting and said that there was no change in the ownership at CBS as yet. ABC ran nothing. CBS managed to report the hard-news headlines. A flustered Dan Rather received word of the outcome just as he was closing his broadcast and managed to give the essential facts (the old leadership of Thomas Wyman was out; Laurence Tisch was now in charge). The next night, 11 September, all three networks offered substantial coverage. CBS's report ran two minutes, the second story on that evening's lineup, following a stock market story by Ray Brady. The veteran political reporter Bruce Morton did the narrative, acknowledging what everyone in broadcasting had been talking about: "Critics in and out of the company had worried that at CBS News, standards were changing, old values eroding in a move toward more entertaining stuff." Morton concluded, "Today the mood was upbeat." A parade of CBS luminaries, both past and present, helped tell a dramatic morality tale: how CBS was getting rid of the bad—CBS president Tom Wyman and news division president Van Gordon Sauter—and replacing it with the good: Tisch, and the trusted old guard of William Paley and Walter Cronkite.

Six months later, Tisch made deep reductions in the CBS News staff, and the morality play looked much less clear-cut. Although CBS News was again in the news, coverage was once again minimal. There were no pictures of its striking writers or fired correspondents. Instead, the image presented was of a television system miming the motions of a serious journalistic enterprise, a system visibly reluctant to dig into a news story that involved news about itself.

There are critics who say that network news covers nothing in depth, so why expect anything different. People in news broadcasting themselves plead guilty to the charge of superficiality. As NBC's Mike Jensen says, "You tell as much as you can tell in two minutes and then assume if they feel the need to know more they'll follow up in print or tune into the "Today" show for a seven-minute interview." ABC correspondent Dan Cordtz concurred: "There's no way that anyone can get all his or her news from television and hope to be even adequately informed." Yet, television news takes time to dally with toys it finds attractive; a Fawn Hall, minor walk-on in the Iran arms scandal, or a Donna Rice, forgettable Miami model linked to a presidential hopeful, warranted more CBS air time in one week than Laurence Tisch received in a year. Another argument often heard is that broadcast-business stories and corporate takeovers cannot be covered by a visual medium. Actually, business-of-television stories have been done regularly, and well, for sizable audiences on the syndicated "Entertainment Tonight." A third argument in defense of television's mishandling of its own business is the cynical one: being a proprietor means never having to say anything about your own business. As the critic A. J. Leibling observed three decades ago, freedom of the press belongs to the man who owns one. In the case of the change of ownership at the networks, ABC, CBS, and NBC tried to stay away from the story of their internal strife until events—and print—forced it onto their agendas. When Congress held three days of hearings on the business of television in the spring of 1987, inviting the new acquisitors of ABC, CBS, and NBC to appear, network news reporters dutifully showed up—to cover "news" that had happened many months before. Even then, value judgments were avoided.

As we saw, the question of how the new owners would influence programming was too quickly dismissed, with wishful assumptions passed off as fact. The bland assurances of 1985 and 1986 evaporated in the late 1980s, at each of the networks. After CBS News dismissed 215 people in March 1987 and cut its budget around 10 percent ($30 million out of an estimated $300 million), there was no longer any reassuring talk about how programming and quality would not be harmed. The coverage was a rerun of the earlier story. Print outlets once again moved ahead with the news before television organizations acknowledged that anything was happening. When Dan Rather displayed his "courage" and spoke out against staff cutbacks and more extreme budget-tightening measures, his forum was a revealing one. He chose to do so in print, on the editorial pages of the *New York Times*, and not on CBS.

The Camera Never (Admits that It) Blinks

22

Too often, television news is not as diligent as it should be in admitting errors and setting the record straight. Three examples: On 12 May 1986 Peter Jennings on ABC's "World News Tonight" introduced some ominous-looking footage of what he described as the damaged Soviet nuclear reactor at Chernobyl. On "NBC Nightly News" for 3 January 1987, in a report looking ahead to the new year and what it might bring for the U.S. economy, chief economics correspondent Irving R. Levine grimly reported that major American companies, including IBM, "plan big layoffs of workers this year." Later that same month, on 30 January, CBS News business correspondent Ray Brady delivered a startling report emphasizing the uncompetitive nature of the U.S. economy. There were shots of bags of trash being emptied from a garbage truck on a pier in New York City. Brady then reported that wastepaper is the "number 1 export sent out of this port to foreign nations." The clear message: while the Japanese and others send VCRs and electronic goods to the United States to deepen our trade deficit, America exports junk.

Different as these three stories were, they have one element in common: all are wrong. ABC's "Chernobyl reactor," which also showed up on NBC, was actually footage of a cement factory in Trieste, Italy. Contrary to what NBC reported, the IBM company was not laying off employees. It had not had a layoff in 50 years. More precisely, IBM was offering incentives for early retirement or for relocation to other IBM plants to employees of an IBM facility being shut down in Greencastle, Indiana. As for CBS News's dismaying account of how the Port of New York had become mainly an exporter of junk, the story could only be true if exports were measured by weight, not by value—as trade is always calculated.

Television news makes mistakes, quite understandably. Errors are an inevitable consequence of the demand that news organizations—print as well as electronic—process thousands of numbers, names, dates, facts, and images every hour under pressure of daily deadlines and the constant need to compress words and pictures into constricted formats. Still, such errors shake readers' and viewers' faith that what they are reading or seeing is as represented; when that confidence is breached, the reader or viewer may go elsewhere. Understandably spurred by increasing concerns about credibility, newspapers around the country in recent years have developed standard techniques for handling errors. Usually newspapers use correction boxes or, in some cases, have editors or omsbudsmen who specialize in investigating and responding to readers' complaints. For their part, magazines have regular letters-to-the-editor pages where mistakes can be addressed. In a 1986 analysis of newspaper correction policies, the Gannett Center for Media Studies in New York found that most papers have policies for correcting their errors "in fixed places . . . making them accessible to readers." The Gannett researchers concluded that, on average, large newspapers publish a correction every other day.

The policies of the television news organizations fall far short of these print standards. My seemingly simple quest to determine both the frequency of factual errors on television news programs and the networks' policies for correcting them proved to be a monumental task. Each network had different policies for assigning responsibility for corrections and indeed for acknowledging the possibility of error. Moreover, corrections policies vary from program to program within a network. At CBS, the more leisurely magazine shows, such as "60 Minutes" and "CBS Sunday Morning," run occasional letters from viewers offering opinions or corrections; meanwhile, complaining viewers are rarely if ever heard from in the highly constricted format of the "CBS Evening News."

Similarly, on ABC, the single-topic show "Nightline" finds it easier to make on-air corrections, and the ABC program "Viewpoint" every few months provides a 90-minute "live forum" allowing selected audiences to express their opinions. But audience talk-back is not the same as editorial take-back. The networks sometimes act as if the problem of mistakes exists solely in their critics' minds. "We make very few errors and are requested to make very few corrections," said Robert Siegenthaler, a vice-president of ABC News. Corrections that do appear on ABC newscasts follow no set patterns, going "wherever it is graceful," according to Siegenthaler. At ABC, corrections may sometimes appear the next time the program airs, or if the mistake happened in a series of reports, then in a subsequent report. Sometimes corrections can come at the end of the same broadcast in which the error has occurred, if caught quickly enough. Siegenthaler could not say how many requests for corrections the network receives each year or how many are actually made. "I don't keep a box score," he said.

At "CBS Evening News," the executive producer at the time, Tom Bettag, made many of the same points. "There's no way to keep track of corrections," Bettag said. "That's like asking how many times do you change copy. We just do it as we need to." CBS News has a written document listing its "production standards." They are quite specific: "It must be clear, in the correcting broadcast, that we are broadcasting a correction." Therefore, the CBS document continues, merely reporting that the original statement has been denied or reading a viewer's error claim is not enough.

The CBS correction report must specifically admit that the denial or the assertion is accurate and that the original statement was in error.

Andrew Freedman, a publicist for the "NBC Nightly News," tried to be helpful when I attempted to find out the average annual number of NBC corrections. "NBC Nightly News," he maintained, has to correct only a couple of mistakes each year. His claim was off the mark, perhaps because of semantics: NBC News has in the past swept together corrections, amplifications, and questions about taste and news judgments into a category with the general title "Letters to NBC News." For a time these "letters" were answered on the air. In one typical broadcast, Tom Brokaw did a two-and-a-half-minute taped report taking up two complaints from viewers, one that NBC may have been too harsh on President Reagan in its coverage of the Iran Contra scandal, and the other that NBC had failed to forewarn viewers when it was about to show footage of a grisly auto accident. No mistake was claimed in either complaint, and none was acknowledged. This letters report was followed by an admission of an NBC error in using the description "Nazi" for someone who, NBC declared, was instead "a former Nazi." But the "Letters to NBC News" format seldom appeared and was quietly abandoned in the late 1980s. Lawrence K. Grossman, president of NBC News at the time, recalled why in a speech in April 1990. "When I was at NBC News, I tried to start a letters-to-the-editor weekly feature [for] members of the public who were critical of our reporting or who wanted to correct particular stories," he told an audience at the dedication of the new Edward R. Murrow School of Communications at Washington State University. "Our star anchors and producers were unalterably opposed to airing such criticism on our own network. They could dish it out, but when it came to receiving criticism, their jaws were made of glass. The weekly letters-to-NBC feature somehow always ended up on the cutting room floor."

Clearly, television news organizations underestimate the need for a system of corrections. The Gannett researchers took as their premise the view of Thomas Winship, a widely respected journalist and a former editor of the *Boston Globe*. Winship argues that nothing is more critical to a news organization than its reputation for accuracy and that nothing establishes that reputation better than the honest, timely, and public admission of errors. Yet when television news makes a mistake, it may or may not be corrected. Far more serious than the individual errors is the networks' continuing stonewalling attitude, reflected in their nonresponse to errors. The key to on-air corrections too often was whether anyone, inside or outside the news organization, was willing to protest vigorously enough. The "Chernobyl reactor" picture, for example, was quickly corrected. After the video had been shown on Italian television, Peter Jennings told his "World News Tonight" audience two days later: "Some sharp-eyed Italian suggested the pictures were really of Trieste, in Italy. In cooperation with the Italian police we made an investigation, and, yes, the video had been taken at Trieste. We were badly misled, we misled you, and as you can imagine we're not very happy about it." Similarly, in an ABC News report on 9 July 1986 on the U.S. Food and Drug Administration's ban on the use of sulfites in vegetables and salads, the accompanying video showed scenes taken at a D'Lites of America salad bar. The D'Lites chain protested immediately to ABC, and the network the next day reported: "D'Lites of America informs us that they do not use sulfites in their establishments."

A strong protest also galvanized NBC to take corrective action after the IBM "layoff" story appeared in early January 1987. James C. Reilly, IBM's director of communications operations, sent a letter to Andrew Freedman on 7 January. On 17 January, news anchor Connie Chung delivered the following correction: "In recent business stories on 'Nightly News,' it was reported that the IBM Corporation plans big layoffs of workers this year and that other layoffs had already been carried out. IBM says it has not laid off any employees in almost 50 years, nor does it have any plans to do so. IBM does acknowledge that 10,000 of its employees have accepted its offer of incentives to retire early." Complaints need not come from a corporate giant if a valid point is involved. On the NBC "Today" show on 22 October 1986, host Jane Pauley discussed the problems of women alcoholics with two experts. Footage of some women at a party—a generic "drinking scene"—briefly introduced the narrative. A few of the women on the tape quite by accident saw the story and complained that they were identifiable. They protested that they were not alcoholics, as the juxtaposition of words and images could be taken to imply. The next morning cohost Bryant Gumbel acknowledged that NBC had been wrong to link the footage with the story.

But not all such wrongs are righted. The CBS "wastepaper export" story was doubly rank. It first surfaced as a "fact" in the Democratic party reply, delivered by the House Speaker Jim Wright (D-Texas), to Ronald Reagan's State of the Union address. Both speeches were televised on 27 January 1987. The idea of junk as New York's leading export proved irresistible; three days later, CBS followed Wright's lead.

Sometimes disputed stories never get straightened out, however forceful the protest. The Atomic Industrial Forum, a nuclear industry lobbying association, engaged CBS News in a correctional battle about a story broadcast on the "CBS Evening News" on 27 August 1984. A French cargo ship, carrying some 250 tons of the nuclear material uranium hexafluoride in sealed containers, collided with a West German ferry and sank to the bottom of the English Channel. CBS News correspondent David Andelman in Paris reported carefully: "How much a pressing environmental danger the cargo . . . represents remains debatable." But in the introduction to the correspondent's report, the CBS anchor, the normally reassuring Bill Kurtis, quoted a spokesperson from the "environmental action group Greenpeace." As Kurtis told it, the Greenpeace man issued a "frightening warning . . . if just one drop of water leaked into the sealed containers of uranium hexafluoride, there could be an immediate violent explosion." Donald Winston, director of media relations for the Forum, immediately asked for a retraction from Howard Stringer, at the time vice-president of CBS News. Winston wrote that CBS News had relied "on the incorrect language" of Greenpeace. Uranium hexafluoride, Winston said, could not explode on contact with sea water. CBS aired subsequent reports on the accident but never corrected its erroneous report, even after the containers were safely recovered.

According to a Roper poll conducted in 1986, 66 percent of Americans cited television as their main source of news: more than half (55 percent) said they think television is the most credible source of news. In contrast, just one in five said they believe newspapers are the most credible news source. These figures are puzzling in light of the way television news handles corrections. Is there a way to explain the relationship between the public's trust in television and television's unsystematic (to be charitable) approach to corrections?

The most straightforward explanation, of course, would be that television is less error-prone, or, putting it another way, sharper and more professional than newspapers. Therefore television does not need daily corrections boxes or special editors in charge of handling complaints. The television system would like to see itself that way. "It's the news staff's job not to make errors," NBC's Andrew Freedman says. Adds CBS's Tom Bettag: "Researchers as well as editors read scripts, make calls, check the facts before they go on the air." But as most television people would be the first to acknowledge, television news is not infallible. More likely, television's credibility exists in part as aura: many viewers apparently believe that "pictures don't lie." The impression that Dan, or Tom, or Peter looks honest may be enough for the unwary. The viewer can also say, "I saw it for myself on TV." At the same time, newspapers have more opportunities for error and a tradition of acknowledging them. Possibly, aura persists in part because television refrains almost automatically from too-frequent challenges to its own credibility through too-frequent acknowledgment of errors.

When the forces demanding redress are formidable—for example, a megacorporation and respected institution like IBM—then the acknowledgment of wrongs may take place gracefully. But news managers may think they can ride out a request for correction because their work disappears into the ether as soon as it flashes on screen; the ephemeral nature of the image tempers any impulse to correct mistakes. Conversely, newspapers may be motivated to greater vigilance in correcting mistakes by their knowledge that they are "organs of record," or aspire to be. It benefits a newspaper in the long run to correct a mistake; it becomes accountable.

If print worries about its accountability, then television is concerned about image. To the degree that television lacks regular, self-contained correction mechanisms in its news programs, the medium is open to accusations of wanting the appearance of credibility rather than credibility itself. Such a stance inevitably places it squarely in the ranks, already swollen, of the dissembling institutions of our day.

You Saw It Here First

23

Early in the evening of 3 January 1990 Manuel Antonio Noriega, the Panamanian general, surrendered to United States authorities, for all practical purposes, on U.S. television.

Around 9:15 P.M. (EST) the networks interrupted their regular programming to report that Noriega had left the Vatican embassy. By 9:30 ABC, CBS, and CNN were showing videotape, shot with nightscope cameras, of U.S. Army helicopters airlifting Noriega to a nearby American base. At 9:40 President George Bush was announcing that all U.S. objectives had been achieved, and CNN began nonstop coverage, going live to U.S. Army general Maxwell Thurman's briefing in Panama. At 11:30, "Nightline" capped the evening's coverage with a 36-minute report; Peter Jennings had an impressive interview with Panama's archbishop, Marcos McGrath, about the days and nights of Manuel Noriega inside the Vatican embassy. The next day viewers could see it all over again on the morning news programs, about the same time newspapers were being delivered to their doorsteps. The question is, What was there left to read?

This is not an abstract issue. Television's Panama show was a preview of the grander Gulf War of January–February 1991. Both media war shows followed an extraordinary run of news tailor-made for TV in the late fall and early winter of 1989: the fall of the Berlin Wall, the candlelight vigils in Wenceslas Square, the revolution in Romania, complete with close-up images of the executed Ceausescu. The worlds that came tumbling down in Eastern Europe, Panama, and the Gulf have also helped turn journalism on its head. What purpose does a morning paper serve, when television gives the news the night before? For that matter, what is the function of the newsmagazines, published days after the event? The role of newspapers and news weeklies has been changing over the past few years; the coverage out of Eastern Europe, Panama, and the Gulf region demonstrates how great the changes have been.

Now that television regularly provides the hard news, newspapers have to present the background information and analysis that used to be the franchise of the news weeklies. And as the dailies take over their techniques, weekly newsmagazines move toward the sort of opinions and essays that once belonged chiefly to monthlies and books. The personal voice has replaced the narrative story line in print outlets. "There's a feeling that the main story is for the record, and that a lot of readers skip it," a senior *New York Times* executive explained to me. "The real effort" at the paper, he adds, "now goes into the accompanying analyses and the related stories." In its Eastern European coverage, for example, the *Times* gave comprehensive chronological reconstructions of the big events, a form known in the newsmagazine trade as "ticktocks" (from the sound a clock makes). Late in 1989, four of the paper's top reporters put together the chronology of Erich Honecker's last days in power in East Germany. In January 1990 another *Times* team produced a ticktock on the final days of the tyrant Ceausescu. In the *Washington Post*, reporter William Branigin offered a dramatic, magazine-style account of a roadblock shootout in Panama City four days before the U.S. attack. Branigin's article appeared on page 1 in the edition of 4 January, just below the hard-news account of Noriega's surrender. While the lead story repeated what viewers had learned from television the night before, Branigin offered fresh information; he showed how a wrong turn in Panama City by a U.S. military driver new to the country may have set the stage for the invasion. "Everyone wants to get beyond the bang-bang people now see on television," says Norman Sandler, a White House correspondent for United Press International. The day after the invasion, when the television networks were describing the prospects for the "swift military defeat" of Noriega, Sandler filed an analysis of the economic and political entanglements the Bush administration was taking on in Panama.

The daily newspapers now borrow heavily from television and from *USA Today* as well as from the weeklies. The New York Times published boxes, reference data, and pronunciation guides about Soviet-bloc countries as they appeared in the news—"user-friendly materials," according to executive editor Max Frankel. Even though not everyone has an opportunity to bring up, in dinner-table talk, the name of the last Romanian political prisoner to be released by the Ceausescu Securitate, the *Times* helpfully explained that Mircea Raceanu's full name is pronounced "meer-CHAY-ah rah-CHYAH-noo." But the *Times*'s efforts did help to remind readers of facts they may have forgotten over the past 40 years of cold war: the total population of Bulgaria (9 million) or the fate of the Moldavians who came under Red Army rule in 1940 (they are today unhappy Soviet citizens).

At the newsweeklies, the television revolution has also changed the way stories are treated. Standard chronologies of events have been displaced; instead, says Maynard Parker, editor of *Newsweek*, "We use a variety of approaches, a bigger bag of tricks." After the Berlin Wall fell, *Newsweek* enlisted Henry Kissinger to ponder the deeper meaning of it all. "We all saw Tom Brokaw earlier in the week, so we had to go on from there," says Parker. When the capture of Noriega also received extensive spot coverage in the middle of the week, *Newsweek*, for its "second day" story, turned to Frederick Kempe of the *Wall Street Journal*, who had been working on an investigative book about Noriega and his reputed ties to the drug cartel, Fidel Castro, George Bush, and the CIA. Kempe helped *Newsweek* preview relevant parts of the book. At *Time*, once the holy grotto of group journalism, Lucestyle has been all but abandoned. In the 1 January 1990 issue, two articles with bylines led the magazine, and the Gorbachev cover story included four signed essays. Michael Kramer's piece was a deft justification of *Time*'s selection of Gorbachev as its Man of the Decade, well written but with little new information. In fact, the magazine's Man of the Year feature has become less a news story than a way of differentiating *Time* from the competition. It represents one thing that television does not yet do.

Television's immediacy has changed much more than the component parts of newspapers and magazines. It has affected the nature of the information being offered as well, and in a way not yet fully understood by the journalists involved in the process. The phrase "visual generation" is not just one of the clichés of our time. The arrival of 1990 produced one of those old standards of journalism, a review of the past decade. Some of the younger researchers who worked on the surveys of the 1980s at the networks expressed their amazement at how much television has changed in ten years. Early news footage—from 1980!—seemed old-fashioned, "almost as if it was in black and white," recalled an associate producer, age 25, at NBC News. In contrast, the contemporary footage appeared to her to be more involving, glossier, "more MTV-like." Newspapers and newsmagazines must now compete directly with television for the patronage of this presumptively visual audience, schooled on "Sesame Street" and music videos. The changes in print are instructive. Pictures in the pages of the *New York Times* in 1990 were larger than they were a year before. In the first four pages of *Newsweek*'s report on the last days of Ceausescu, there were ten columns of pictures to two columns of text. "We harkened back to *Life* magazine," says Maynard Parker.

Everyone now wants to see the world as it is—in color. The newsmagazines have expensive equipment to ensure color photography of the latest events. The *Times* is spending $500 million to build a new printing plant, in part to get color capability for its pages. None of this will change the new facts of media life. Most people get their first news from television. Newspapers will never look like music videos, even if they should want to. Editors have to go where television will not go, or can not go: to explanation, analysis, point of view. For what it is worth, here is one reader's experience reading the newspapers on the morning of 4 January 1990. I skipped right through the Noriega coverage I had seen the night before. Then I read the *New York Times*'s 1,500-word story in the "Home" section about the designer Bran Ferren, who helped build his own high-tech house in the country. Among other features, the house boasted sensors to close the windows and skylights when it rains. It was one story I had not already seen on television.

Index

Abbott, Jack, 162
ABC. *See also* ABC News; Capital Cities/ABC; Jennings, Peter; "World News Tonight"
  corrections in, 205, 207
  documentaries of, 32–33
  on 1988 election debates, 179
  and remake of news operations, 15–17
  strikes at, 13
  takeover of, 16–17, 18, 197, 198, 199
ABC News. *See also* ABC; Capital Cities/ABC; Jennings, Peter; Koppel, Ted; "Nightline"; "World News Tonight"
  and entertainment shows, 41–42
  on hostages, 135–138
  innovative techniques at, 32
  in 1960s, 40
ABC News/*Washington Post* poll, 176
ABC Sports, 42
Abrams, Robert, 105–106
Addato, Kiku, 185
AIDS, sex, and good taste, 75–86, 87–92
Ailes, Roger, 186
Akihito, Emperor, 158
Alda, Alan, 29
Allen, Marcus, 30
Alter, Jonathan, 188
Altschuler, Alan, 165
Amal militia, 134, 135, 136–137
"America for Sale" (CBS), 160
Amsterdam News, 118
Amusing Ourselves to Death: Public Discourse in the Age of Show Business (Postman), 169
"Analytical reporting," 15
Anchormen, TV, 37–54
  defined, 39–40
Andelman, David, 210
Andropov, Yuri, 150
Annals of Internal Medicine, 75
Annenberg School of Communications (U. of Pennsylvania), 29
"Antidocumentary," 31
Arbitron, 51–52
Arledge, Roone, 11, 12, 15–17, 42, 65, 67
Arts and Entertainment network, 35
Associated Press, 91
Astor, Brooke, 166
Atlanta Journal-Constitution, 174, 179

Atlantic, 165
Atomic Industrial Forum, 210–211
Audubon Society, 35
Aug, Stephen, 199
Auld, Meredith. *See* Brokaw, Meredith

Baker, Russell, 190
Barrett, Rona, 167
Barry, Marion, 124
"Battle for Asia-Thailand, The" (NBC), 33
Bazell, Robert, 52, 80–81, 85–86
"Bear in the Woods" commercial, 144, 149
"Before and After Midnight" (Gostelradio), 5
"Behind Party Lines" (CBS), 146
Benjamin, Burton, 29, 32, 35, 36
Berlin Wall, 148, 213
Bernstein, Leonard, 47
Berri, Nabih, 137
Bettag, Tom, 207–208, 211
Bias, Len, 96–97
Biden, Joseph, 174, 176, 177, 180
Black Tar heroin, 95
Blind Date, 155
Blood transfusions, and AIDS, 79–80
Bloomingdale, Betsy, 161
Boesky, Ivan, 124, 200
Boston Globe, 80, 134, 179, 209
Bradshaw, Thornton, 51
Brady, Ray, 198, 201, 202, 205
Branigin, William, 214–215
Brawley, Glenda, 101, 103–111
Brawley, Tawana, 101, 103-111
Brezhnev, Leonid, 4, 142, 150
Brinkley, David, 40, 150, 184
Briscoe, Michael, 119
Brokaw, Meredith, 51
Brokaw, Tom, 19, 20, 24–25, 30, 100, 190, 198, 215
on CBS change, 201
on cocaine, 97
and corrections, 208
coverage of AIDS, 75, 77
on crack, 96
expanded interview role of, 17–18
and "NBC Nightly News," 50–54
public image of, 37–39
and Rather, 51
on U.S.-Japan trade, 154
as White House reporter, 42
work habits of, 38
Brown, Tina, 91
Browne, Jackson, 36
Bruno, Hal, 187
Buchanan, Patrick, 113–114
Buckley, William F., Jr., 168
Bumpurs, Eleanor, 104
Burke, Daniel, 16
Burnett, Carol, 163
Burns, George, 170
Bush, Barbara, 163
Bush, George
and Campaign '88, 185–187
as candidate, 177
and Gorbachev, 148, 149–151
on Japan, 158
on Noriega, 213
relations of, with press, 189–193

Cabey, Darrell, 107
Cable News Network (CNN), 54. *See also* CNN
Cable television, 21, 35–36
Camera Never Blinks, The (Rather), 43
Campaign '88, 183–188
media and, 177–178
Canadian Broadcasting Company (CBC), 48, 55
Capital Cities/ABC, 16
Capital Cities Communications, and ABC takeover, 197, 198, 199

Capra, Frank, 32
Carter, Jimmy, 178
Cavazos, Lauro, 192
CBNC, 22
CBS, 183. *See also* "CBS Evening News"; "CBS Morning News"; Rather, Dan
  change in command of, 200–203
  corrections in, 205, 206, 207–208
  documentaries of, 32–33
  and '88 debates, 179
  strikes at, 13
  on RCA takeover, 200
  takeover of, 12, 13–15, 16
"CBS Evening News," 5, 24–25, 56, 100. *See also* CBS; "CBS Morning News"; CBS News; Rather, Dan
  on ABC takeover, 198
  on AIDS, 77
  and Bush, 189–190
  change in command of, 197–198, 201–202
  and Rather, 43–46
  streamlining of, 14–15
  on TWA hijacking, 130, 132
"CBS Morning News," 56
  on TWA hijacking, 130, 132, 133–134
CBS News, 154, 210–211
CBS News/*New York Times* poll, 187, 193
"CBS Reports," 32, 33
Ceausescu, Nicolae, 214
Celebrity deaths, AIDS and, 87–92
Central Park jogger, coverage of, 113–122
Chancellor, John, 50, 62, 99, 138
"Character issue," 174, 184
Chase, Rebecca, 95
Cher, 170
Chernenko, K. U., 150

Chernobyl, nuclear reactor disaster at, 4–5, 139–141, 205, 209
Chicago Sun-Times, 180–181
Chicago Tribune, 143, 150, 186
Chung, Connie, 29, 99, 209–210
City Sun, 118–119
Clymer, Adam, 177
CNN (Cable News Network), 24, 55–63, 123, 124, 180, 183
  appraisal of, 60–63
  coverage of, 12, 15, 56–63
  and '88 debates, 179
  on Japan, 159
  and networks, 62
  on Noriega, 213
  programs of, 13
  on TWA hijacking, 132
"Cocaine Country" (NBC), 99
Cohen, Richard, 113
Cohn, Roy, 87, 90, 91
Colangelo, Robert, 116
Color, as trend in news, 216–217
"Conventional Wisdom, The," 186
Conwell, Allyn, 135
Coopers & Lybrand, 12
Cordtz, Dan, 202
Cosby, Bill, 35, 50
Costello, Frank, 125
Couric, Katherine, 24
Cousteau, Jacques, 35
Crack, coverage of epidemic of, 93–100
Cronkite, Walter, 35, 162, 202
  as protoanchor, 39–41
  and Rather, compared, 45–46
"Crossfire" (CNN), 119
Cuomo, Mario, 77, 105
Cutler, Bruce, 126

Dallas Morning-News, 179
Daniels, Faith, 24
Davis, Larry, 107

"Daybreak" (CNN), 55, 56, 59–60, 62
Deaver, Michael, 161, 191
De Giovanni, David, 100
Delta Force, 131, 133
Demjanjak, John, 14
Dennis, Everette, 176
Derickson, Uli, 137
Derwinski, Edward, 192
Des Moines Register-Tribune, 174, 179
Detente, 142–144, 149
Dewey, Thomas, 187
"Dial market share," 22
Diaz, David, 103
Dinkins, David, 105, 170
Discover magazine, 83
D'Lites of America, 209
Documentaries, TV, 29–36
Dolan, Christine, 61
Dolan, John Terrence "Terry," 87, 88–89
Dole, Robert, 184
Donahue, Phil, 34
Donaldson, Sam, 65–69, 121, 129
Downey, Morton, Jr., 22
Drago, Ivan, 147
Drew, Robert, 32, 33
Drinan, Robert, 62
Dukakis, Michael, 173, 175, 177, 180
  and coverage of campaign of, 183, 185, 187
Duke, David, 69
Dukes, Hazel, 104

Eagleton, Tom, 175
"Early Frost, An" (NBC), 75
Ebenezer Baptist Church, 106
Ebersole, Dick, 19–20, 23
Editorial commentary, 62
Edward R. Murrow School of Communications (Washington State University), 208

Ellis, Perry, 87, 90, 91
Errors, techniques for handling, 206

Fairness in Media group, 200
Falwell, Jerry, 62
Fauci, Anthony, 79
Fenton, Tom, 146
Ferren, Bran, 217
Fierstein, Harvey, 87
"Fishbowl, the," 44
Flaherty, Robert, 32
Flaste, Richard, 85
Flint, Julie, 135
Ford, Betty, 163
Ford, Gerald, 178
Ford, Henry, 170
"48 Hours" (CBS), 31, 35, 66
"48 Hours on Crack Street," 31, 99
Fox network, 20
Frank, Reuven, 34
Frankel, Max, 174–175, 215
Freedman, Andrew, 208, 209, 211
Friendly, Fred, 32
"Frontline" series (PBS), 35

Gannett Center for Media Studies (Columbia University), 176, 206
Gans, Herbert J., 164
Garagiola, Joe, 19, 20, 24
Garth, David, 165, 170
Gartner, Michael, 19, 22–23
General Electric, 197, 199–200
Geneva summit, TV coverage of, 58, 60, 142
Gerasimov, Gennady, 58
Gitlin, Irving, 32
Glasnost, 148
Glass, Charles, 134, 135
"God and Politics" (PBS), 36
Goetz, Bernhard, 108
Goldman, John, 124, 126
Goodell, Rae, 167

"Good Evening Moscow" (Gostelradio), 5
"Good Morning America" (ABC), 56, 136
Gorbachev, Mikhail, 3, 125, 191
 coverage of speech of, 3–4
 at Geneva summit, 58, 60
 as Man of Decade, 148–151, 216
 and Reagan, 142
Gorbachev, Raisa, 58
Gore, Albert, 178
Gosnell, Mariana, 83
Gostelradio, 4, 6, 7, 8
Gotti, John, 123-127
Grady, William, 104-105
Graham, Jim, 79
Grahan, Katherine, 162, 163
Greene, Lorne, 33
Greenfield, Jeff, 184, 187-188
Greenpeace, 210-211
Greenspun, Hank, 89
Gregorian, Vartan, 166
Grierson, John, 32
Griffith, Michael, 104
Grossman, Lawrence K., 22, 30, 149, 208
Grossmayer, Simon, 135-136
Gulf War, TV coverage of, 11-12, 57-58
Gumbel, Bryant, 19, 20, 81, 210
"Gung Ho," 155
Guzman, Pablo, 123, 126

Haidar, Akif, 135
Haitian connection, 76, 80
Handelsman, Steve, 25
Hard news
 on CNN, 59
 defined, 6
 Soviet, 6–7
Harper, Pat, 82
Hart, Gary, 173, 176, 180
 and '88 campaign, 184–185

Hartman, David, 135–136, 137
"Harvest of Shame" (CBS), 32, 39
Hawn, Goldie, 29
Heiskell, Andrew, 166
Heller, Joseph, 163
Helms, Jesse, 200
Helmsley, Leona, 124, 127
Hendrie, Joseph, 141
Henig, Robin Marantz, 78
Hewitt, Don, 33, 69–70
Hill, Pamela, 35
Hirohito, Emperor, 158
Hoge, James, 110
Holcomb, Theodore, 143
Honecker, Erich, 214
"Honey shots," 42
Howard Beach case, 120, 125
Hudson, Rock, 76, 77, 87
Hume, Brit, 193
Huntley, Chet, 40
Hussein, Saddam, 154
Hynes, Charles, 105, 110

Iacocca, Lee, 170
IBM, incorrect layoff story on, 205-206, 209-210
Iglesias, Julio, 126
Informational programming, 34–36
"Infotainment," 34, 39
Ingrassio, Angelo J., 106
Iran-Contra scandal, 166
Irish Republican Army (IRA), 106, 110
"It's a Dog's World" (NBC), 33

Jackson, Jesse, 105, 169, 174, 176, 177
 campaign of, 180–181, 184
Jackson, Keith, 67
Japan, and United States, 153–160
Japan, Inc., 153, 155
Jarriel, Tom, 99
Jenkins, Carol, 82

Jennings, Peter, 24–25, 96, 97, 137–138, 159
  and Campaign '88, 184
  on CBS changes, 201
  and corrections, 205, 209
  and hostage interview, 136
  on Noriega affair, 213
  profile of, 46–49
  public image of, 37–39
  on strike, 198
  on TWA hijacking, 130–132
Jensen, Mike, 199, 201, 202
Johnson, Derwin, 135
Johnson, Lyndon B., 41, 178
"Just Say No" crusade, 95

Kayal, Philip, 82
Kemp, Jack, 189
Kempe, Frederick, 215–216
Kennedy, John F., 178, 193
Khrushchev, Nikita, 150
King, Ralph, 103
Kinnock, Neil, 174
Kinsley, Michael, 166, 175
Kissinger, Henry, 132, 165–166, 177, 215
Kladstrup, Don, 134
"Knot's Landing" (CBS), 66, 67
Koch, Ed, 77, 164, 170
Koppel, Ted, 18, 54, 66, 105. *See also* "Nightline"
  on TWA hijacking, 132
Kramer, Michael, 216
Krevchenko, Leonid P., 9
Kriegel, Mark, 127
Kunstler, William, 107
Kurtis, Bill, 210
Kurtz, Howard, 124

"L.A. Law" (NBC), 66, 67, 71
Langone, John, 83
Language, level of in media, 82–86
"Larry King Live" (CNN), 56

Las Vegas Sun, 89, 90
"Late Night" (NBC), 197
Laufer, Peter, 79
Lazutkin, Valentin, 7
Leacock, Richard, 32
Lederer, Elizabeth, 116
Lehrer, Jim, 18
Leibling, A. J., 203
Letterman, David, 197
"Letters to NBC News," 208
Levine, Bettijane, 91
Levine, Irving R., 205
Lewis, George, 159
Liberace, 87, 89–90, 91
Life, 76, 216
Lippman, Walter, 141, 179
"Little Lisa" case, 124, 125
Loew's Corporation, 200
London *Times*, 164, 183
Long-form specials, 31. *See also* Documentaries
Lord, Bill, 46
Lorentz, Pare, 32
Lorik, Oscar, 61
Los Angeles Times, 78, 87, 124

McFarlane, Robert, 166
McGovern, George, 144, 175
McGrady, Phyllis, 67
McGrath, Archbishop Marcos, 213
Mack, Joseph, 119
McKay, Jim, 67
McKinnon, Perry, 108–109
McKinsey & Company, 12, 17–18
MacNeil, Robert, 18
"MacNeil/Lehrer News Hour" (PBS), 54, 186
Maddox, Alton H., Jr., 102, 107, 109, 110, 119
Magid, James, 200
Mailer, Norman, 162
"March of Time, The" (Time Inc.), 32

Margolis, Jon, 185
Marijuana, 96
Marton, Kati, 37
Mason, C. Vernon, 102, 105, 107, 109, 110
May Day parade, coverage of, 8–9
Media, as moral police, 173–181
Medved, Miroslav, 59
Medvedev, Roy, 6
Medvedev, Sergei, 8, 9–10
"Meet the Press" (NBC), 56
Metropolitan Edison of Pennsylvania, 141
Miami Herald, 179, 180
Midas Muffler commercial, 147–148
Milken, Michael, 124
Miller, Don, 159
Miller, John, 123, 125–126
Mine Shaft, 81–82, 83
Molchanov, Vladimir, 5
"Moneyline" (CNN), 56
Morgenthau, Robert, 107
Morrisroe, Patricia, 91–92
Morton, Bruce, 202
Moscow News, 58
Moscow on the Hudson, 147
Mother Jones, 53
Moyers, Bill, 36, 62
Mudd, Roger, 95, 136, 137
Murdoch, Rupert, 164
Murphy, Dennis, 96
Murphy, Mary, 126
Murphy, Tom, 16, 198
Murrow, Edward R., 32, 39

Nachman, Jerry, 84
Nader, Ralph, 163, 199
National Association for the Advancement of Colored People, 104
National Enquirer, 87
National Geographic Society, 35
National Journal, 176

National Youth Movement, 108
NBC, 19-25, 183. *See also* Brokaw, Tom; "NBC Nightly News"
  documentaries of, 32–33
  and '88 debates, 179
  strikes at, 13
  takeover of, 12, 17, 197, 199–200
  on TWA hijacking, 130, 132
"NBC Nightly News," 24–25, 56. *See also* Brokaw, Tom; NBC
  on ABC takeover, 198–199
  appraisal of, 50–54
  on Biden, 174
  on CBS takeover, 301
  on cocaine, 97
  corrections of, 205, 208, 209–210
  on crack, 96
  decline of, 20, 24
  remaking of, 17–18
  on Russian economy, 146
  on U.S.-Japan trade, 154
NBC Radio, 79
"Negro Revolution, The" (NBC), 33
Neilsen surveys, 30, 38, 43, 51–52. *See also* Arbitron; Polls; Public opinion polls; Roper poll
Nelson, Harry, 78
Network evening news
  and anchormen, 39–54
  and CNN, 59–60, 62
  of future, 18
  pre-1980s, 12
  and takeovers, 12–18
Nevins, Barbara, 123
Newfoundland crash, 55, 56–57
New Republic, 166, 168, 175
"Newsbreak" (CBS), 130
Newscasts
  labor-management strife in, 13
  response of, to errors, 209

Index   225

Newsday, 81–82, 87, 108, 115, 117, 123
"News Hour" (PBS), 18
News programs, cost of prime time, 66
Newsweek, 82, 87, 135, 142, 188
 on Campaign '88, 186
 on CBS changes, 201
 coverage of, 215–216
New York Daily News, 109, 110, 123
 on AIDS, 81
 on Brawley case, 103
 on "wilding," 116
New York Law Journal, 109–110
New York magazine, 92
New York Post, 115, 123
New York Public Health Council, 81
New York Public Library, 166
New York Review of Books, 168
New York Times, 68–69, 87, 110, 111, 115, 154, 177, 183, 190, 192
 on AIDS, 77–80, 85
 on Biden, 174
 on Campaign '88, 186
 on Central Park jogger, 115, 117
 changes in, 216, 217
 on "character issue," 174–175
 coverage of, 214, 215
 on Dolan story, 89
 as forum, 203
 on Jesse Jackson, 174
 on Liberace, 90
 on Moscow Book Fair, 145
 on Muscovites, 146, 147
 on Soviet culture lag, 143
 on Soviet gerontocracy, 150
"Nightline" (ABC), 13, 18, 25, 54, 56, 66. *See also* ABC; ABC News; Koppel, Ted
 on Brawley case, 105
 corrections on, 207
 and documentary themes, 34
 impact of, 180
 on Noriega, 213
 on TWA hijacking, 132
"90 Minutes" (NBC), 34
Nixon, Richard M., 142–144, 163, 178, 183
Noonan, Peggy, 186
Noriega, Manuel Antonio, 213
Norville, Deborah, 19, 20, 24
Nuclear Regulatory Commission, 141
"Nyetnashe," 8–9

O'Connor, John F., 123
"Octobriana," 143
On-air chemistry, 69
Onassis, Jacqueline Kennedy, 162, 164
"120 Minutes" (Gostelradio), 5
Operation Blast Furnace, 98–99
Overinterpretation, of Campaign '88, 184
Ownership, changes in, 202–203

Paley, William S., 12, 202
Palmer, John, 23–24
Parker, Maynard, 215, 216
Patterson, Basil, 105
Pauley, Jane, 19, 20, 210
 and change at NBC, 23–24
Payne, Daniel, 173, 178
PBS, documentaries on, 35–36
Pearson, Richard, 90–91
People magazine, 87, 180
Perestroika, 148, 195–217
Perry, Matthew, 158
Perry, William "The Refrigerator," 166–167
"Person of the Week" (ABC), 47–48, 49
Phillips, Mark, 145–146
Pienciak, Richard, 109
Pizzey, Allen, 52

Index 226

Plisetskaya, Maya, 3
Poindexter, John, 166
Polls. *See also* Arbitron; Neilsen surveys; Public opinion polls; Roper poll
 in Campaign '88, 182
 as media-made news, 187
Postman, Neil, 169
Poussaint, Alvin, 116
Presser, Jackie, 48
"Primenews" (CNN), 56, 58, 59
"Prime Time Live" (ABC), 65–71
Process vs. substance, 186
Pryor, Richard, 95
Public opinion polls, 186–187
Public sex, 77
Public TV, documentaries on, 35–36

Quayle, Dan, 184
Quinones, John, 48, 98, 100

Raceanu, Mircea, 215
Raines, Howell, 192
Rambo, 147
Rather, Dan, 24–25, 159, 190, 198
 and "CBS Evening News," 43–46
 on CBS takeover, 201, 202, 203
 on crack, 93–94
 and Cronkite, compared, 45–46
 on hostage interview, 136
 public image of, 37–39
 and streamlining of operations, 14
 on terrorists, 134
 as White House reporter, 42
Rather, Irwin "Rags," 43
Ratings, 51–52
RCA, takeover of, 197, 199–200
Reagan, Ronald
 and Geneva summit, 58, 142
 image of, 165, 178–179
 relations of, with press, 191–192
 and State of the Union address, 210

Reagan, Nancy, 50, 58
 anti-drug crusade of, 95
 image of, 161–162
Reckoning, The (Halberstam), 156
Red Dawn, 147
Reilly, James C., 209
Reston, James, 179
Reynolds, Frank, 46
Rice, Donna, 184–185
Riney, Hal, 144
Rivera, Geraldo, 22, 123
Robertson, Marion G. "Pat," 174, 175–176, 177
 campaign of, 180, 184
Rocky IV, 146–147
Rogers, Don, 97
Rohatyn, Felix, 162, 168
Romania, revolution in, 213–214
Roper poll, as news source, 211
Rose, Judd, 67, 69
Rosen, Richard, 110
Rosenberg, Eliyahu, 14
Rubenstein, Howard, 166
Russell, Cristine, 84
Russert, Timothy, 100

Sagalaev, Eduard, 7
Sagan, Carl, 167
Sagan, Paul, 104
Saint James, Susan, 20
Salinger, Pierre, 16
Sanders, Jonathan, 5
Sandler, Norman, 215
Santucci, John, 105
Sarnoff, David, 12
Sasso, John, 180
"Saturday Night Live" (NBC), 169
Sauter, Van Gordon, 44, 202
Sawyer, David, 173, 177, 180
Sawyer, Diane, 65–68
"Scared Sexless" (NBC), 29–30
Schieffer, Bob, 132
Schneider, William, 176

Schorr, Daniel, 61
Schultz, George P., 139, 192
"Secret Government... The Constitution in Crisis, The" (PBS), 36
Seligmann, Jean, 83
"Seven Days" (Gostelradio), 6
Shadows of the Rising Sun, 156
Sharpton, Reverend Al, 101, 107, 108, 111, 114, 119
Sherr, Lynn, 184, 198
Shiite Moslem terrorists, 134
Shipler, David, 147
Shriver, Maria, 19, 20, 30
Siegal, Allan M., 89, 90, 92
Siegenthaler, Robert, 207
Silverman, Fred, 41–42
Simon, Bob, 14
Simon, Paul, 175
Sims-Phillips, Anna, 108–109, 119
"60 Minutes" (CBS), 13, 33, 66, 91
Sloan, Alfred P., 170
Smirnoff, Yakov, 148
Smith, Dorrance, 67
Smith, Terence, 132
Snyder, Tom, 50
Soft news, 6
 defined, 7
Soviet Union
 American image of, 142–151
 television of, 5
Speakes, Larry, 59
Spielberg, Steven, 163
Stahl, Lesley, 133, 181
Stallone, Sylvester, 146–147
Steinberg, Joel, 124, 125
Steinbrenner, George, 164
Steinem, Gloria, 163
Stern, Henry J., 115
Stethem, Robert, 131, 134
Stewart, Michael, 104
Streamlining, at CBS News, 14–15

Strikes
 at ABC, 198
 at NBC, 13
Stringer, Howard, 11, 13, 14–15, 211
Stuart, Charles, 120
Sununu, John, 190

Taibbi, Mike, 103, 106, 108–109, 111
Takeshita, Noboru, 158
"Tanya" commercial, 143–144
Tate, Sheila, 161
Taubman, Philip, 146
Taylor, Paul, 173
Television
 changes in, 20–21, 54, 216–217
 lack of accountability in, 212
Television diplomacy, complaints re, 137
Television stations, independent, 21
Terrorvision, 129–138
Testrake, John, 131, 135
Theory Z, 156
"They Have Souls, Too" (ABC), 35
"This Week with David Brinkley" (ABC), 113, 116
Thornburgh, Dick, 141
Thorson, Scott, 89
Three Mile Island, accident at, 140–141
Threlkeld, Richard, 145
Thurman, Maxwell, 213
"Ticktocks," 214
Tillman, Rosa, 117
Time, 87, 168
 coverage of, 216
 on Gorbachev, 149
 on hostages, 135
 on Russians, 142
Time, Inc., 32
Tinker, Grant, 20, 200

Tisch, Laurence, 13–14, 165, 198
  as head of CBS, 200–202
"Today" (NBC), 13, 56
  changes in, 21, 23–24
  decline of, 20
  and documentary themes, 34
Tokyo Broadcasting System, 154
Trade imbalance, U.S.-Japan, 157
Truman, Harry S, 187
Trump, Donald, 114, 165
Turner, Ted, 35, 55–56, 63, 200
TWA 847 hijacking, 129
"Twentieth Century, The" series (CBS), 32, 35
"20/20" (ABC), 30, 33, 66
"Twin Peaks" (ABC), 20, 25

"U-2 Affair, The" (NBC), 32–33
Unholy Alliances: Working the Tawana Brawley Story (Taibbi/Sims-Phillips), 119
United Parcel Service commercial, 154–155
United Press International, 80, 215
United States, and Japan, 153–160
Uranium hexafluoride, 210–211
USA Today, 87, 180, 183, 215
U.S. Center for Disease Control, 86
U.S. Drug Enforcement Administration, 100
U.S. National Institute on Drug Abuse (NIDA), 95
U.S. National Institutes of Health, 79, 91
U.S. News and World Report, 165
  on Chernobyl, 139
  on Japanese, 155
USSR, images of, 139–151. *See also* Soviet Union
U.S.S. Stark, 154
Utley, Garrick, 146

Vanity Fair, 91
VCR ownership, impact of, 21
"View" (Gostelradio), 5–6
Viewers, share of, 20–21
"Vremya" (Gostelradio), 3
  programs of, 5–6, 7–11
  and soft news, 7

Wald, Richard, 69
Wallace, Chris, 67
Wallace, Mike, 91, 181
Wall Street Journal, 174, 180, 181, 183, 215–216
Walters, Barbara, 66
Warren, Robert Penn, 163, 168
Washington Post, 87, 88, 89, 124, 179, 180, 183
  on AIDS, 80
  and Bush, 190, 192
  on Central Park jogger, 113
  coverage of, 214–215
  and Gary Hart, 173
  and Gorbachev, 191
  on language, 84
  obit policies of, 90–91
  and Watergate, 162
Washington Redskins, 191
Washington Times, 87–88
Wastepaper export story, 205, 210
Watts, Rolanda, 82
WCBS, 103, 108, 110
Weinberger, Caspar, 193
Welch, John, 21, 199
Wenceslas Square, vigils in, 213
Wendy's hamburger commercial, 148
"West 57th" (CBS), 33
Westin, Av, 15–16, 30–31, 32, 49
Wheatley, Bill, 21
White, Theodore, 179
"White Paper" programs (NBC), 32, 33

Index   229

Whitmoyer, Claude, 131
Whitney, Helen, 35
"Why We Fight" series, 32
Wicker, Tom, 190
Wilder, Douglas, 170–171
"Wilding," defined, 116
Will, George, 58, 116, 130, 135
Williams, Mary Alice, 57
Willis, Bruce, 155
Willse, James, 81, 83–84
Winfrey, Oprah, 34
Winship, Thomas, 209
Winston, Donald, 211
WLIB radio, 118
WNBC, 82
Woodward, Robert, 173
"World News Tonight" (ABC), 24–25, 56, 137, 197. *See also* ABC; ABC News; Jennings, Peter
  on ABC takeover, 198, 199
  on American image in the USSR, 145
  on CBS change in command, 201, 202
  corrections in, 205, 209
  and Peter Jennings, 46–48
  on RCA takeover, 200
  remaking of, 15–17
  on Russian culture, 146
  on Shiite Moslems, 134
  on TWA hijacking, 130–131
  on war on drugs, 95–99
Wright, Jim, 210
Wright, Robert, 17, 19, 22
WTBS, documentaries on, 35
Wyman, Thomas, 201, 202

"Yanqui, No!" (NBC), 33
Years of Upheaval (Kissinger), 177
Yeutter, Clayton, 192

Zipkin, Jerome, 161
Zolotarevsky, Leonid, 4
Zuckerman, Mortimer, 165